BYOB

CHICAGO

Your Guide to
Bring-Your-Own-Bottle
Restaurants and
Wine & Spirits Stores
in Chicago

 **2nd** Edition

Jean Iversen

BYOB Chicago

Your Guide to Bring-Your-Own-Bottle Restaurants and Wine & Spirits Stores in Chicago, 2nd Edition

by Jean Iversen

Copyright © 2007 by BYOB Chicago, Inc.

BYOB Chicago[SM] is a servicemark of BYOB Chicago, Inc.

First Printing

Publisher, Author: Jean Iversen
Contributors: Mark Child, Ray Daniels, Joe Kafka, Larry Mechanic
Proofreading: Whitney Ward
Interior Design: Emily Brackett, Visible Logic, www.visiblelogic.com
Cover Design, Logo: Emily Brackett, Visible Logic
Maps: Wendy Miranda
Photography/Images: Lukasz Bernas (page 127), Junji Takemoto (page 129), Ian McDonnell, www.ianmcdonell.com (back cover)

Printed in the United States of America
ISBN 0-9764131-1-6
978-09764131-1-0

BYOB Chicago, Inc.
P.O. Box 477803
Chicago, IL 60647
www.BYOB-Chicago.com

All of the information in the listings has been provided or confirmed by the restaurants and wine & spirits stores in this book, and BYOB Chicago, Inc., assumes no responsibility for errors, inaccuracies, omissions, or any inconsistencies herein. This book continues to be developed without any unnecessary meetings, conference calls, emails, or text messages.

Contents

Publisher's Note

Writing the first edition of *BYOB Chicago* provided me with a great introduction to many undiscovered restaurants and boutique wine shops in Chicago. But publishing *BYOB Chicago* was another story—I never expected such a tremendous response. Nearly 10,000 copies of the book sold—not only in Chicago, but all over the country—testifying to the appeal of BYOB dining to locals and out-of-towners alike.

BYOB dining in Chicago is not only popular but a trend that will continue to grow. I've uncovered nearly 100 more BYOB restaurants since the last edition. *100 more.* Plus, Chicagoans on average consume more wine than most other U.S. cities, fueling the BYOB trend further. More Chicagoland restaurants have BYOB or no-corkage nights. There are more wine clubs, wine tastings, wine bars, wine classes, and wine festivals in Chicago, and there's increased media coverage on BYOB dining and wine in general.

Most major U.S. cities cannot boast a thriving BYOB dining scene. In the majority of states, taking your own bottle of alcohol to a licensed or unlicensed restaurant is illegal. Even in areas of the country where it is allowed, such as California wine country, restaurants tend to prohibit BYOB so they can sell their own wine list. Let's face it: when it comes to cities that allow diners to BYOB, Chicago is king. Here, BYOB is not only legal, it's encouraged and celebrated.

It's my joy to present the second edition of *BYOB Chicago*. Not only are there almost 250 BYOB restaurants for you to choose from, there are also listings of over 60 shops that sell boutique wines and premium beers and spirits.

I would like to thank those who contributed to this new and improved edition: Emily Brackett, Whitney Ward, Erika Johnson, Mark Child, Larry Mechanic, Joe Kafka, Ray Daniels, Wendy Miranda, and Peter Schwarzbach. Thank you for helping me pull this great guide together and for giving it a lot of unexpected surprises that I know will be valuable to readers. I would also like to thank my friends and family—especially Mom and Dad for their support and entrepreneurial spirit.

I hope you enjoy this edition even more than the first. As always, I welcome your feedback and thank you for making *BYOB Chicago* one of the most popular dining guides in Chicago.

Cheers!

Jean Iversen
Publisher
info@byobchicago.com

How to Use This Guide

This is the second edition of *BYOB Chicago*. There have been many changes since the first one, which published in February 2005. Nearly 100 new BYOB restaurants opened, several closed, and there was an explosion of new wine stores in both the city and the suburbs. This edition contains these updates as well as many new features that should make this guide even more useful when navigating the BYOB dining scene in Chicagoland.

About This Book

While many changes have occurred since the last edition, the way this book is written is essentially the same. To gather the information for the "BYOB Restaurants A–Z" section, I personally visited each and every restaurant. I confirmed with restaurant owners and staff that they had no plans to apply for a liquor license. Those who stated they had plans to apply for one, or who were waiting for their liquor license application to be approved, or were in the process of selling their restaurant, were not included in this book. Therefore, there are no "temporary BYOBs" in this book.

However, there are some exceptions. I did include one restaurant that was in the process of getting a liquor license but will continue to accommodate BYOB diners afterward (Coast Sushi Bar). I also included a few restaurants that have been waiting so long for their liquor licenses that it's a safe bet you can BYOB there for the long haul (State Restaurant and Café, Sweet Tamarind, Zen Noodles). There are also a couple that have been saying for years that they're going to get a liquor license but haven't (Bamboo Garden, Thai Classic), as well as a few that are on the fence and may be applying sometime in 2007 (Indie Café, Butterfly Sushi Bar & Thai Cuisine, Pingpong).

Rest assured that all the other restaurants in this book are either BYOB by default (city ordinances, only one bathroom, located in a dry district) or design (owner wants to focus on the food, having a liquor license is too costly, owner's religion forbids alcohol, BYOB policy attracts more customers). These restaurants not only allow but encourage their clientele to BYOB.

Some restaurants charge a modest service fee, or corkage fee, to cover their costs for glassware and Champagne buckets or to compensate for the fact that you're not ordering a beverage from their menu. The restaurant listings in this edition indicate when a restaurant does not charge any corkage fee.

Changes to the Second Edition

It seems that more and more restaurants in Chicago are forgoing a liquor license in the interest of attracting a growing population of BYOB diners. Even restaurants who have a full bar are responding to this trend by offering BYOB or no-corkage nights. Others allow BYOB any night of the week but charge a corkage fee for this courtesy. These corkage fees can range from $5–$50 a bottle. In this edition, I include many of these restaurants in "Restaurants That Allow BYOB for Corkage Fees of $15 or Less." This list includes a who's who of restaurants in both the city and the suburbs, from Highland Park to Oak Park and all points in between. I think you'll be pleasantly surprised at the breadth of options out there. Before you go, check out "BYOB Etiquette at Licensed Restaurants" so that you're more prepared.

In the "BYOB Restaurants A–Z" section, I added information on the type of beverage service and glassware each restaurant offers. Some restaurants, like Think and Kan Zaman, provide full beverage service and open your wine bottles, chill them, offer a full range of stemware, refill your glasses, etc. Other restaurants do not have so much as a corkscrew. That's fine—as long as they're not charging corkage.

Lastly, I've expanded the book to include BYOBs from the northwest side, south side, Chinatown, Evanston, Oak Park, and Pilsen.

New Features

Joe Kafka, owner of KAFKA wine co. in Lakeview, returns to impart his wisdom with a "Pairing Wine with Food" chart. Not to slight those who love to bring a brew to BYOBs, Ray Daniels has also returned with a "Pairing Beer with Food" chart. Both experts provide excellent tips on what wine or beer pairs with a wide range of foods and flavors. These are well worth browsing.

You may notice a huge increase in the number of sushi BYOBs in this edition. The sushi trend seems to be far from over in Chicago. Why not use this as an excuse to explore the great, new sakes on the market? Sales-wise, sake is the fastest-growing spirit in America, and nothing goes down smoother or pairs better with sushi or sashimi than a great sake. In "Sake 101," expert Larry Mechanic explains the basics of sake and how to select the perfect bottle.

In "Wine & Spirits Stores A–Z," you will be tripping over a list of more than 60 great wine shops located in Chicago and the suburbs. If you feel like a deer in the headlights at wine stores, you may want to check out two articles: "Wine Labels Decoded," by Mark Child, to assist you in decipher-ing that gibberish on the label; and "10 Questions to Ask at Your Local Wine Shop," by Joe Kafka.

In response to favorable feedback, I have included the "BYOB Restaurants by Cuisine" and "BYOB Restaurants by Neighborhood" indexes again. I added a "BYOB Restaurants by Feature" index, which lists BYOBs that feature outdoor seating or live entertainment. Speaking of live entertain-ment, there is also a brief list of non-restaurant BYOB venues in "Off the Beaten Path BYOBs." It's a Chicago tradi-tion to laugh it up at a midnight improv theater with your own six-pack. Now you can find not only BYOB improv theaters but also hookah lounges, cafés, and more.

Newcomers and Closings

This edition features a list of restaurants even more impres-sive than the last. There are many new promising Mexican BYOBs, for example, that offer a contemporary twist on traditional Mexican cuisine. Returning favorites are Caliente and Rique's Regional. Newcomers Los Nopales, Dorado, and Sol de Mexico are also making waves with customers and critics and are worth checking out.

Italian BYOBs seem to be in high demand. I'm happy to report several great restaurants in this category; returning are Think, Caro Mio, La Cucina di Donatella, and Lucia Ristorante, as well as newcomers Terragusto and Pizza Rustica. Trattoria Caterina in the South Loop seems to be hitting its stride, as well.

There are more upscale BYOBs than you may think. While Tango Sur, Speakeasy, Think, May St. Café, Rick's Café Casablanca, Friendship Restaurant, and a few others have been around for a while, a table at the newly opened HB, Terragusto, and Schwa also gives foodies a chance to BYOB.

We must say farewell to some BYOBs since the last edition: Thai Little Home Café, Ann Sather in Wicker Park, Leo's Lunchroom, Privata Café, Ambassador Café, Café Demir, Country Smoke House, Anatolian Kabob, Muang Thai, Lovitt, Mamacita's in Lakeview, Sonargaon, Blue Cactus, and others. Others missing from this edition have either received or applied for their liquor licenses.

While all of the information was current as of press time, some of the details may change throughout the life of this edition. However, barring any exceptions noted above, all of the restaurants in this book ensured *BYOB Chicago* that they would remain BYOB at least until the end of 2007.

If you know of a BYOB that is not in the book but should be, please send an email to info@byobchicago.com so that I can have the opportunity to list it in the next edition.

Enjoy this second edition of *BYOB Chicago!*

—J.I.

BYOB
Restaurants

CHICAGO

Key to Symbols Used

PRICES

$ = average entrée costs $6–$8
$$ = average entrée costs $9–$14
$$$ = average entrée costs $15–$20
$$$$ = average entrée costs over $20

SYMBOLS

Ⓟ   Parking available

⚑   Outdoor seating

♪   Live entertainment

ATM   ATM on premises

OTHER

YOYO = "You're On Your Own" (restaurant does not furnish glasses, corkscrews, or any type of beverage service)

BYOB
Restaurants A–Z

ADESSO $$
3332 N. Broadway (Aldine), Lakeview
Brunch/Italian
Adesso is taking over the old Einstein's Bagels location in Lakeview.
Expect Sicilian favorites, a kid's menu, and weekend brunch.
(773) 868-1516, www.eatadesso.com, Mon–Thurs 10:30–10:30,
Fri 10:30–11:00, Sat 8:30–11, Sun 8:30–10:30

AFGHAN RESTAURANT $$
2818 W. Devon (California), West Rogers Park
Afghan/Vegetarian-Friendly
New management took over this casual, bright storefront and
embellished the menu with more veggie options. For carnivores,
the lamb shank, with marinated onions, chickpeas, and rice, is a
popular dinner entrée. They provide wine glasses and corkscrews.
No corkage fee.
(773) 262-8000, www.afghankabobhouse.com, 11:30–late night
every day Ⓟ

ALWAYS THAI $
1825 W. Irving Park Rd. (Ravenswood), North Center
Thai
The food is made with love here by a chef/owner that spent seven
years at Arun's. Enjoy perfectly balanced flavors, especially in the
moo ping's barbecue sauce and succulent chive dumplings. The
soothing yellow walls and cute atmosphere provide respite from
bustling Irving Park Road (except on Friday nights, when they
break out the karaoke). They provide wine glasses, beer mugs, ice
buckets, and corkscrews. No corkage fee.
(773) 929-0100, Mon–Thurs 11–9:30, Fri 11–10, Sat 1–10, Sun
4–8:30 ♪

ANDALOUS MOROCCAN $$
3307 N. Clark (Belmont), Lakeview
Moroccan/Vegetarian-Friendly

Tagines—slow-cooked Moroccan stews—are the highlight here.
These delicious concoctions of vegetables and complex herbs
and spices are cooked in clay pots with beef, lamb, chicken, or
seafood (vegetarian options also available) until the meat falls
off the bone. Shishas (hookas) are available. They provide wine
glasses and open your bottles. No corkage fee.
(773) 281-6885, www.andalous.com, Mon–Thurs 4–10, Fri 4–12,
Sat 11–12, Sun 11–10, reservations recommended every night ⟨⟩

ANN SATHER $$
929 W. Belmont (Clark), Lakeview
Scandinavian/American/Brunch

Many American dishes have been added to the menu, and the
upstairs party room is now home to a comedy club at this original
location. One thing that remains? The mouth-watering cinnamon
rolls, a Chicago classic. They provide wine glasses, Champagne
flutes (there's orange juice for mimosas), and beer mugs. No
corkage fee.
(773) 348-2378, www.annsather.com, Mon–Tues 7–3, Wed–Sun
7–9 Ⓟ

ANN SATHER $$
3411 N. Broadway (Roscoe), Lakeview
Scandinavian/American/Brunch

If grooving to Donna Summer while noshing on eggs and toast
is your thing, this location offers "disco brunch" the first Sunday
of every month. On days that you don't want to indulge while
wearing spandex, this is a pretty relaxing environment to enjoy
weekend brunch or weekday breakfast and lunch. They provide
wine glasses and ice buckets. No corkage fee.
(773) 305-0024, www.annsather.com, Mon–Fri 7–3, Sat–Sun 7–4

ANN SATHER $$
3416 N. Southport (Roscoe), Lakeview
Scandinavian/American/Brunch
This location does not serve dinner, but they do offer the same breakfast and lunch menu as the other two locations, as well as a great outdoor space to enjoy some people watching along the now-trendy Southport corridor. They provide wine glasses. No corkage fee.
(773) 404-4475, www.annsather.com, 7–3 every day 🖝

AROY THAI $
4656 N. Damen (Leland), Ravenswood
Thai
The aroy noodle (rice noodles with BBQ pork, plum sugar, and ground peanuts) and cashew noodle (cashews, onions, pineapple, stir-fried noodles) are highly recommended here. They provide wine glasses, pint glasses, and corkscrews. No corkage fee.
(773) 275-8360, 11–10 every day

ASIAN AVENUE $$$
1624 W. Belmont (Ashland), Lakeview
Sushi/Japanese/Thai
Former Sushi Wabi and Tsunami sushi chef Alan Julamoke opened this bright, contemporary spot in summer 2006 to excellent reviews. The menu includes Julamoke's mother's Thai recipes as well as sushi, maki, and Japanese entrées. They provide red and white wine stemware, sake cups, and ice chillers and will heat up your sake in hot water. No corkage fee.
(773) 549-2201, Mon–Thurs 11:30–10, Fri–Sat 11:30–11, Sun 11:30–9

AT CAFÉ $
2739 W. Touhy (California), West Rogers Park
Thai
This recently opened neighborhood spot serves all the standard Thai favorites in a casual setting. They provide wine glasses, pilsner glasses, and corkscrews. No corkage fee.
(773) 338-9533, Mon–Sat 11–9, Sun 4–9

ATLAS CAFÉ $$
3028 W. Armitage (Humboldt Blvd.), Logan Square
Café/Eclectic/Vegetarian-Friendly
Husband-and-wife team Youssef and Isabel Abbadi preside over
this new casual café. The menu has Mexican, South American,
and Italian influences. BYOB is especially popular on nights with
live entertainment (call for a schedule). They provide wine glasses
and ice buckets upon request. No corkage fee.
(773) 227-0022, 11–10 every day ♬

AY AY PICANTE $$
4569 N. Elston (Wilson), Mayfair
Peruvian
There are beaucoup seafood items and nightly specials at this
well-kept secret on the northwest side. Diners especially love the
ceviche de pescado (tilapia in lime juice with Peruvian potatoes,
sweet potatoes, onions, and corn). They provide wine glasses,
corkscrews, and ice buckets. No corkage fee.
(773) 427-4239, www.ayaypicante.com, Mon–Thurs 11–10:30,
Fri–Sun 11–11

AZHA $
960 W. Belmont (Sheffield), Lakeview
Thai
This is a bare-bones, casual place to grab classic Thai fare on
your way to other destinations in the heart of Lakeview. Diners
especially rave about the crab Rangoon, pad Thai, village steamed
dumplings, and pot stickers. They provide wine glasses, Champagne flutes, pilsner glasses, ice buckets, and corkscrews. No
corkage fee.
(773) 525-0555, Mon–Thurs 11–10, Fri–Sat 11–11, Sun 4–9

BQ AFRO ROOT CUISINE $$
4802 N. Clark (Lawrence), Uptown
African
Husband-and-wife team Briggs and Queen are at the helm of this
popular West African restaurant. It's mostly a takeout joint but
allows BYOB in the casual dining room. They have corkscrews on
hand. No corkage fee.
(773) 878-7489, Mon–Sat 11–10, Sun 12–10

BA MIEN VIET FOOD COURT $$

4941 N. Broadway (Argyle), Uptown
Vietnamese/Chinese/Vegetarian-Friendly

This is an experience, not a restaurant! Vietnamese artifacts hug
the walls and hang from the ceiling, and a huge karaoke screen
beckons from the stage. Free parking after 7 next door. They have
wine glasses, Champagne flutes, brandy glasses, ice buckets, and
corkscrews on hand. No corkage fee.

(773) 878-8811, Mon closed, Tues–Thurs 10–10, Fri–Sun 10–11
Ⓟ ♫

THE BAGEL $$

3107 N. Broadway (Briar), Lakeview
Jewish/American

A family institution for over 50 years, The Bagel offers Jewish and
American entrées, complete or a la carte. (And you can't beat the
free parking lot in back.) They have juice and water glasses on
hand for your wine or beer and will provide corkscrews or open
your wine bottles upon request. No corkage fee.

(773) 477-0300, www.bagelrestaurant.com, Sun–Thurs 8–10,
Fri–Sat 8–11 Ⓟ ᴀᴛᴍ

BAMBOO GARDEN $

3203 N. Clark (Belmont), Lakeview
Chinese/Vegetarian-Friendly

Nothing fancy here, just a traditional mix of Chinese favorites,
available in large or small portions. There are, however, an impressive number of seafood offerings, such as the "Lucky Shrimp
Family." They've anticipated getting a liquor license for years, but
nothing has materialized yet, so your bottle of Pinot Grigio is safe
from corkage for now. Beverage service: YOYO.

(773) 525-7600, 11–11 every day

BARBERRY PAN ASIAN KITCHEN $

2819 N. Southport (Diversey), Lakeview
Thai

This tiny kitchen cranks out an impressive takeout and delivery
business, but there's also a 14-seat, private dining room upstairs—something about it makes you feel like you're sneaking
away from a boring party. They provide corkscrews upon request.
No corkage fee.

(773) 525-6695, 11–10 every day

BEN TRE CAFÉ & RESTAURANT $$
3146 W. Touhy (Kedzie), West Rogers Park
Vietnamese
The bright-green walls provide an instant energy boost as you walk into this small, casual spot. The menu consists mostly of Vietnamese pho and noodle, rice, and seafood dishes (plus a few Chinese offerings). They provide wine glasses and corkscrews upon request. No corkage fee.
(773) 465-3011, Sun–Tues 11–9:30, Wed closed, Thurs 11–9:30, Fri–Sat 11–10 Ⓟ

BHABI'S KITCHEN $$
6352 N. Oakley (Devon), West Rogers Park
Indian/Pakistani
Owners Qudrat and Bhabi Syed provide the best home-cooked Indian food around in an ever-expanding dining room. The naan with pistachio and mixed dry fruit is worth the trip. They provide red and white wine stemware, pilsner glasses, Champagne flutes, rocks glasses, ice buckets, and corkscrews. No corkage fee.
(773) 764-7007, 12–11 every day, reservations recommended every night

BITE CAFÉ $$
1039 N. Western (Augusta), Ukrainian Village
Eclectic/Vegetarian-Friendly/Brunch
The menu features delicious, healthy cuisine. The specials rotate every couple of days, but the regular menu includes a falafel plate, spaghetti arrabiata, and beer-battered catfish. If you want an alcoholic beverage, simply walk through the door that connects Bite to the bar next door, The Empty Bottle. There you can purchase wine, draft microbrews, bottled beer, or mixed drinks until about 8:30, then walk back to your table, drinks in hand. The Empty Bottle offers four types of red wine and three types of white, by the glass or bottle, at very reasonable prices. Check out www.emptybottle.com/about.htm for their "booze" menu. If you bring your own, Bite has juice glasses and corkscrews on hand. No corkage fee.
(773) 395-2483, www.emptybottle.com/bite.htm, Sun–Thurs 8–10:30, Fri–Sat 8–11:30

BLUE ELEPHANT $

1235 W. Devon (Magnolia), Edgewater
Pan-Asian

New owners have refocused the menu on pan-Asian cuisine, so
expect such dishes as blackberry salmon, pineapple salmon curry,
and imperial shrimp (light, vermicelli-wrapped rolls in a delicate
apricot sauce). They provide fancy schmancy wine goblets,
pilsner glasses, martini glasses, and corkscrews. No corkage fee.
(773) 262-5216, www.blueelephant2g.com, Sun–Fri 11–10, Sat
4–9 ✒

BON SOIREE $$$

2728 W. Armitage (California), Logan Square
Eclectic/Brunch

Bon Soiree calls itself an "upscale delicatessen." Their deli
offerings were so popular they started serving them for breakfast,
lunch, dinner, and weekend brunch. French, Asian, and other
influences appear on the dinner menu (grilled rack of lamb with
Japanese eggplant, Grand Marnier–seared salmon with Spanish
tortilla and roasted portabella mushrooms). They provide wine
glasses and corkscrews. No corkage fee.
(773) 486-7511, www.bon-soiree.com, Mon–Fri 11–8:30, Sat–Sun 9–4

BORINQUEN $$

1720 N. California (Bloomingdale), Humboldt Park
Puerto Rican

Authentic Puerto Rican fare is the highlight at this family-friendly
restaurant, known as "home of the jibarito," a sandwich made
with beefsteak and fried green plantains. Check out their bilingual
Web site; it's chock full o' information. Beverage service: YOYO.
No corkage fee.
(773) 227-6038, www.borinquenjibaro.com, 10–10 every day

BUENA VISTA RESTAURANT $$

3147 N. Broadway (Briar), Lakeview
Mexican

This cute, 24-seat eatery in Lakeview serves made-to-order, traditional Mexican, from tacos and tortas to sautéed shrimp in white
wine and garlic sauce. Their complimentary tortilla chips and spicy
salsa always start things off in the right direction. They provide
wine glasses and corkscrews upon request. No corkage fee.
(773) 871-5782, Mon–Sat 11–11, Sun 11–10

BUENOS AIRES FOREVER $$
939 N. Ashland (Augusta), Noble Square
Argentinian
On a busy strip of Ashland, this new storefront features *parrillada*,
a traditional Argentinian grill on which customers prepare their
own cuts of meat, sausages, and sweet breads. There are appetizers
and salads for herbivores and hot or cold sandwiches under eight
bucks. They provide wine glasses and corkscrews. No corkage fee.
(773) 486-8081, Mon–Thurs 10–9:30, Fri 10–10:30, Sat
8:30–10:30, Sun 8:30–9:30

BUTTERFLY SUSHI BAR & THAI CUISINE $$
1156 W. Grand (Racine), River West
Sushi/Thai/Japanese
A young, hip crowd packs this River West sushi and Thai place—if
not for the cool, contemporary atmosphere, then for the high-quality,
reasonably priced sushi (the fish is ordered daily). They provide wine
glasses, Champagne flutes, and sake cups and will warm up your
sake in the microwave (good luck getting an ice bucket when it's
busy). No corkage fee.
(312) 563-5555, www.butterflysushi.com, Mon–Thurs 11–10, Fri
11–11, Sat 12–11, Sun 12–10, reservations recommended 🗦

BUZZ CAFÉ $$
905 S. Lombard (Harrison), Oak Park
American/Café/Brunch
This is a quintessential neighborhood café, right down to the locally
produced art for sale on the walls. There are nightly dinner specials;
a recent stop found barbecued pork chops and mashed sweet
potatoes on the menu. Brunch on Sunday only. They provide wine
glasses and martini glasses and will open wine bottles upon request.
No corkage fee.
(708) 524-2899, www.thebuzzcafe.com, Mon–Fri 6a–9,
Sat 7a–9, Sun 8–2 🗦

CAFÉ BLOSSOM $$
608 W. Barry (Broadway), Lakeview
Sushi/Japanese

At this cute neighborhood gem, you can't go wrong with the
sashimi cervichi (salmon, tuna, and yellowtail topped with spicy
mayo, avocado, and seaweed) or tataki salad (greens and seared tuna
with sesame). They provide wine glasses, sake cups, sake bottles,
and corkscrews and will put your bottles in the cooler or warm
up your sake in the microwave upon request. No corkage fee.
(773) 935-5284, Mon–Sat 4:30–11, Sun 12:30–11 ⚑

CAFE CENTRAL $$
1437 W. Chicago (Noble), West Town
Puerto Rican/Caribbean

This family-run neighborhood institution has served traditional,
homestyle Puerto Rican cuisine since 1950. The menu includes
a large number of seafood-laden dishes. While only a handful
BYOB here, it is welcome. They provide styrofoam cups for wine
and plastic cups for beer. No corkage fee.
(312) 243-6776, 9–9 every day

CAFÉ COREA $$
1603 E. 55th (Cornell), Hyde Park
Korean

This small, spartan, but cute place serves authentic Korean dishes
such as kimchi and bulgogi from an open grill. Few BYOB here
(they had to run upstairs for a wine glass when asked for one),
but it is allowed. They provide the aforementioned stemware and
corkscrews upon request. No corkage fee.
(773) 288-1795, Mon–Fri 11:30–9, Sat 12–9, Sun closed

CAFÉ FURAIBO $$
2907 N. Lincoln (Diversey), Lakeview
Sushi/Japanese

While most of the business here is takeout or delivery, you can
enjoy sushi, maki, katsu, or teriyaki in contemporary, minimalist
surroundings. They provide wine glasses, pint glasses, and
sake cups and will warm up your sake in the microwave. No
corkage fee.
(773) 472-7017, www.cafefuraibo.com, Mon–Thurs 11:30–10, Fri
11:30–11 (closed from 2:30–5 Mon–Fri), Sat 5–11, Sun 4–9

CAFÉ HOANG $
1010 W. Argyle (Sheridan), Uptown
Vietnamese/Thai
If you can get past the lackluster décor, the pho (beef noodle soup), thin soups, and rice noodle with shrimp are all standouts here. They provide wine glasses upon request. No corkage fee.
(773) 878-9943, Mon–Sat 10–10:30, Sun 10–10

CAFÉ LAO $
1007 W. Argyle (Sheridan), Uptown
Vietnamese
This bright, cozy noodle shop would be a more promising BYOB option if the owners didn't insist on charging a corkage fee of $5–$10 per bottle (for parties of 4 or more). They have some wine glasses on hand, and servers will open your bottles.
(773) 275-5094, Fri–Wed 10–11, Thurs closed

CAFÉ SOCIETY $
1801 S. Indiana (18th), Prairie District
Eclectic
Located in the stunning National Vietnam Veterans Art Museum in the Prairie District, this café seats 100 in the outdoor courtyard and about 50 more between the indoor café and dining room across the hall. The menu features all-day breakfast and daily seafood and steak specials. They provide wine glasses, ice buckets, and corkscrews. No corkage fee.
(312) 842-4210, Sun–Wed 7a–5, Thurs–Sat 7a–11

CAFÉ SUSHI $$
1342 N. Wells (Evergreen), Old Town
Sushi/Japanese
The school across the street (actually, it's a fence that belongs to the school) prevents this place from obtaining its liquor license. They provide wine glasses, pint glasses, and ice buckets and will warm up your sake upon request (no sake cups; "The sake bombers broke them.") No corkage with a $15 minimum food purchase per person in parties of six or more.
(312) 337-0700, Mon–Sat 11:30–9:30, Sun 1–9, reservations recommended on weekends ✈

CAFÉ TOO $$
4715 N. Sheridan (Leland), Uptown
Eclectic/Brunch

Students at this café's 13-week culinary skills job training program
cook and serve tempting dishes in a Zen-like atmosphere. They
provide wine glasses. No corkage fee.
(773) 275-0626, www.inspirationcorp.org, Mon 7–10a, Tues–Wed
7a–3p, Thurs–Fri 7a–9p, Sat 9–9, Sun 9–3 🌂

CAFÉ TRINIDAD $$
557 E. 75th (Rhodes), Chatham
Caribbean

The menu here features cuisine from Trinidad and Tobago, which
has a mixed bag of influences, including Jamaican, Caribbean,
African, and Creole. Highlights include callaloo (creamy spinach
and okra), red snapper, and roti wraps. They provide wine and
beer glasses, ice buckets, and corkscrews. No corkage fee.
(773) 846-8081, www.cafetrinidad.com, Mon–Thurs 11–8, Fri–Sat
11–9, Sun 12:30–7

CAFFE FLORIAN $$
1450 E. 57th (Blackstone), Hyde Park
Italian/American/Brunch

A popular spot for locals and University of Chicago students to
enjoy weekend brunch, gourmet pizzas (artichoke pesto anyone?), and entrées such as three-cheese lasagne. Locally produced
art and exposed brick walls contribute to the funky ambience.
They provide small rocks glasses and corkscrews. No corkage fee.
(773) 752-4100, www.florianchicago.com, Mon–Thurs 11–10:30,
Fri–Sat 11–12, Sun 10–11

CALIENTE $$
3910 N. Sheridan (Irving Park Rd.), Lakeview
Mexican

This is Mexican with a contemporary twist—chicken in mole
sauce and flaky empanadas top the list. The staff could not be
more accommodating—they'll mix your margaritas in the kitchen
(as long as you bring the tequila and the mix), add rim salt, and
even throw in a lime for good measure. They also have wine
glasses and servers will open your bottles. No corkage fee.
(773) 525-0129, Sun–Mon closed, Tues–Thurs 5–10, Fri–Sat 5–11 🌂

CALIENTE $$$
2556 W. Fullerton (Rockwell), Logan Square
Mexican

This is chef/owner Vicky Medina's recently opened second location. Expect the same contemporary Latin flavor in the atmosphere and food, but in a much larger and loungier space. Call ahead to confirm their hours, beverage service, BYOB policy, and corkage fee.

(773) 525-0129, open for lunch and dinner

CALVIN'S BBQ $$
2540 W. Armitage (Rockwell), Logan Square
BBQ

St. Louis–born chef Calvin Woods serves up hickory-smoked barbecue at this casual, busy spot. Ribs, pork, chicken, beef brisket, shrimp—you name it—are smoked and served with succulent barbecue sauce and comfort-food sides. They provide plastic cups and there's a corkscrew hanging on a nail in the dining room; otherwise YOYO. No corkage fee.

(773) 342-5100, www.calvinsbbq.com, Mon–Thurs 11:30–9, Fri–Sat 11:30–10, Sun 12–9 Ⓟ 🚩

CARACAS GRILL $$
6340 N. Clark (Devon), Rogers Park
South American

The bright, yellow-colored walls lend a Caribbean feel to this family-run Venezuelan restaurant, which opened in 2004. They provide red and white wine stemware, pint glasses, ice buckets, and corkscrews.

(773) 262-9900, Mon closed, Tues–Fri 5–10, Sat 12–11, Sun 12–9

CARO MIO ITALIAN RISTORANTE $$$
1827 W. Wilson (Wolcott), Ravenswood
Italian/Vegetarian-Friendly

The gorgeous ambience and diverse menu make this a great celebration destination for 2 or 40. They provide wine glasses, rocks glasses, Champagne flutes, wine chillers, Champagne buckets, and servers will open your wine. No corkage fee.

(773) 275-5000, www.caromiochicago.com, Mon–Thurs 11–10, Fri 11–11, Sat 4–11, Sun 3–9, reservations recommended (only taken for parties of 6 or more) 🚩

CASBAH CAFÉ $$$
3151 N. Broadway (Briar), Lakeview
Middle Eastern
This charming eatery (too small to accommodate a bar, thus no liquor license) features excellent Middle Eastern cuisine. The beef kibbeh is out of this world, and a wide variety of couscous, pasta, and rice entrées make for mouth-watering options. They provide wine glasses and whatever else you need. "Just bring your bottles and we'll take care of the rest," says staff.
(773) 935-3339, Mon 5–11, Tues–Thurs 12–11, Fri–Sat 12–12, Sun 12–11

CEDAR'S MEDITERRANEAN KITCHEN $$
1206 E. 53rd (Woodlawn), Hyde Park
Mediterranean/Vegetarian-Friendly
Many unexpected surprises greet you upon entering this establishment: the elegant, contemporary ambience; the open-grill kitchen; and a comprehensive menu that includes dishes not always found at Mediterranean restaurants. Located in Kimbark Plaza. They provide wine glasses, ice chillers, and corkscrews. No corkage fee.
(773) 324-6227, 11:30–10 every day, reservations recommended on weekends Ⓟ

C'EST SI BON $$
5225 S. Harper (52nd), Hyde Park
American/Brunch
This breakfast-and-lunch-only spot is an extension of Renee Bradford's catering business. The sign out front, "sit much and talk long," speaks for the pace here. So go ahead—linger with that bottle of red or white as you feast on the Cajun-influenced cuisine. They provide wine glasses, Champagne flutes, and corkscrews.
(312) 363-4123, Mon–Sat 8-4, Sun 11–3

CHARLEY THAI PLACE $$
3209 W. Armitage (Kedzie), Logan Square
Thai
Cute, cozy spot for authentic Thai in an up-and-coming section of
Logan Square. Favorites are the fried rice and many seafood and
duck entrées. They provide red and white wine stemware, pilsner
glasses, Champagne flutes, and ice buckets. No corkage fee.
(773) 278-3200, www.charleythai.com, Mon closed, Tues–Thurs
11–9:30, Fri–Sat 11–10, Sun 4–9:30

CHIC CAFÉ $$$$
361 W. Chestnut (Orleans), River North
Eclectic
This café is run by the Cooking and Hospitality Institute of
Chicago (CHIC), now affiliated with Le Cordon Bleu. Students
prepare, cook, and serve the food under faculty supervision.
Dinner is a prix fixe menu for $25; lunch is $15 for prix fixe or
$8–$15 for a la carte. They provide wine glasses, pilsner glasses,
and ice buckets and will open your bottles. No corkage fee.
(312) 873-2032, www.chic.edu, Mon–Fri 8–9 (breakfast), 12–1
(lunch), 7:30–8:30 (dinner), Sat–Sun closed

CHINA CAFÉ SEAFOOD RESTAURANT $$
2300 S. Wentworth (23rd), Chinatown
Chinese
You can enjoy dim sum for breakfast, lunch, and dinner here in
the heart of Chinatown. This place is clean, spacious, and food
is served family style (i.e., on lazy Susans in the middle of the
tables). They provide water glasses. No corkage fee.
(312) 808-0202, 8–12 every day

CHINOISERIE $$$
509 4th (Linden), Wilmette
Chinese
Chinoiserie refers to an artistic style with Chinese influences. That
aptly describes the menu at this upscale, 60-seat place in affluent
Wilmette. While the menu has a foundation in Chinese cuisine,
other Asian—and European and Latin—influences also appear.
They provide wine glasses, beer glasses, Champagne flutes, and
corkscrews. No corkage fee.
(847) 256-0306, 4:30–9:30 every day ✎

COAST SUSHI BAR $$$

2045 N. Damen (Armitage), Bucktown
Sushi/Japanese

This popular Bucktown spot recently expanded to accommodate the young, hip crowds that flock here for the consistently fresh sushi and modern, romantic décor. Liquor license is pending; however, they will "continue to accommodate BYOB diners." They provide wine glasses, sake cups, sake pitchers, and ice buckets. They will open your bottles and warm your sake in the microwave. No corkage fee with minimum purchase of $15 (pretax) of food per person.

(773) 235-5775, www.coastsushibar.com, Mon–Sat 4–12, Sun 4–10, reservations recommended every night

COLD COMFORT CAFÉ $

2211 W. North (Leavitt), Wicker Park
American/Jewish/Brunch

Slightly off the beaten path is this friendly neighborhood gem, which serves reliable, excellent breakfast and lunch without the fanfare (or long wait) of other breakfast spots in the Bucktown/Wicker Park area. BYOB is not common here, but it is welcome, especially for weekend parties or brunch. They provide water glasses and corkscrews. No corkage fee.

(773) 772-4552, Mon closed, Tues–Sat 8–4, Sun 9–3 🖐

COZY NOODLES & RICE $

3456 N. Sheffield (Addison), Lakeview
Pan-Asian

The life-sized Elvis clues you in to the fun attitude at this Lakeview eatery, where customers dine at refurbished sewing-machine tables and are greeted with Pez dispenser–covered walls in the women's bathroom. The menu features a slightly contemporary take on mostly Thai cuisine. They provide rocks glasses and ice buckets, and servers will open bottles. No corkage fee.

(773) 327-0100, www.cozychicago.com, Sun–Thurs 11–10, Fri–Sat 11–10:30 Ⓟ 🖐

COZY NOODLES & RICE $
1018 Davis (Maple), Evanston
Pan-Asian
The owners' collectibles fetish is apparent at this second location
in downtown Evanston, where they serve made-to-order Thai and
other Asian noodle and rice dishes. They provide rocks glasses
and ice buckets, and servers will open bottles. No corkage fee.
(847) 733-0101, www.cozynoodles.com, Mon–Thurs 11:30–9:30,
Fri–Sat 11:30–10, Sun 4–9:30

CREPES ON BROADWAY $$
2932 N. Broadway (Oakdale), Lakeview
Crepes/Brunch
At first glance, this new spot in Lakeview appears to be a casual
café, but a second look reveals a full menu of crepe entrées and
desserts. They have a few wine glasses on hand, Champagne
flutes (there's OJ for mimosas), pint glasses, and corkscrews and
will put your bottles in the cooler. No corkage fee.
(773) 248-3622, Sun–Thurs 12–10, Fri–Sat 10–11

CURRY HOUSE $$
2415 N. Clark (Fullerton), Lincoln Park
Indian
If a restaurant filled with customers in the middle of a weekday
afternoon—a rainy one, at that—is any indication of its quality,
this place is top-notch. Satish Muddamalle (who owned Masala
on Devon) offers traditional Indian cuisine in a small, casual spot
along a busy strip of restaurants and shops. They have water
glasses and corkscrews on hand. No corkage fee.
(773) 883-5270, Mon–Fri 12–11, Sat–Sun 12–12

DORADO $$$
2301 W. Foster (Oakley), **Ravenswood**
Mexican

If beautiful décor and swanky atmosphere are musts for your
dining excursions, this might not be your place (in fact, the
exterior is downright ugly). But if your priority is upscale, unique
cuisine, Dorado is an excellent find. Chef/owner Luis Perez
blends French and contemporary Mexican cuisines and achieves
divine results. Nachos get topped with smoked duck; poblano
peppers are stuffed with shrimp, crab, and scallops; and quesadillas are made with whole wheat tortillas, portabella mushrooms,
goat cheese, and roasted tomatillo sauce. Premixed margaritas
are allowed. They provide wine glasses, rocks glasses, margarita
glasses, limes, rim salt, and ice buckets. Servers will open your
bottles and put your beer in the fridge upon request.
(773) 561-3780, www.doradorestaurant.com, Mon closed, Tues–
Thurs 5–10, Fri–Sat 5–11, Sun 5–10, reservations recommended
every night Ⓟ

DRAGON KING $$
2138 S. Archer (Cermak), **Chinatown**
Chinese

For around 10 bucks, you can fill up on northern Chinese
mainstream fare (moo shu pork, shrimp chop suey) or more
unusual plates (lamb, turnip casserole, sliced pork with jellyfish).
The upstairs party room seats up to 150. Located in the Chinatown Square. They provide water glasses. No corkage fee.
(312) 881-0168, Sun–Thurs 11–10, Fri–Sat 11–11:30

DUCK WALK $
919 W. Belmont (Sheffield), **Lakeview**
Thai

In an area where casual Thai restaurants abound, this one is a
standout—the food and cheery service are worth the small,
somewhat cramped space. They provide wine glasses, ice buckets,
and corkscrews, and servers will open wine bottles upon request.
No corkage fee.
(773) 665-0455, www.duckwalkchicago.com, Sun–Thurs 11–10,
Fri–Sat 11–11

ECCE CAFÉ $$
3422 N. Broadway (Roscoe), Lakeview
Pan-Asian/Sushi

With a church and a school nearby, it's no wonder Ecce Café is
BYOB. This cozy restaurant has contemporary décor, a few seats
at the sushi bar, and sidewalk seating for people-watching in the
warmer months. They provide wine glasses, tea cups for sake
(watch those portions), and corkscrews and will heat up your sake
in the microwave and put bottles in the fridge. No corkage fee.
(773) 244-9331, www.eccecafe.com, Mon–Fri 4–11, Sat–Sun
12–11 🐾

EDWARDO'S $
1321 E. 57th (Kenwood), Hyde Park
Italian/Pizza

This is a good, casual place to settle into a booth, crack open a
beer, and feed your deep dish pizza cravings. Folks have been
doing just that since 1978. The menu also features sandwiches
and salads. They provide corkscrews. No corkage fee.
(773) 241-7960, www.edwardos.com, Sun–Thurs 11–10,
Fri–Sat 11–11

EL LLANO RESTAURANT $$
3941 N. Lincoln (Irving Park Rd.), Lakeview
South American

Both locations specialize in chicken, chicken, and—you guessed
it—more chicken, served Colombian style (rotisserie). Diners also
load up on fried plantains, casava, and potatoes. They provide
wine glasses. No corkage fee.
(773) 868-1708, 11–10 every day

EL LLANO RESTAURANT $$
7018 N. Clark (Lunt), Rogers Park
South American
(773) 338-0531, 11–10 every day

EL PRESIDENTE $$
2558 N. Ashland (Wrightwood), Lincoln Park
Mexican
You get a lot of bang for your buck here. The food is authentic,
delicious, and homemade, and the portions are enormous. Plus,
they're open 24 hours a day for those late-night cravings (check
out the midnight-munchie specials from 11–5). They provide
plastic cups; only beer and wine are allowed. No corkage fee.
(773) 525-7938, open 24 hours every day 🐾

THE ELEPHANT $
5348 W. Devon (Central), Edgebrook
Thai
This new Thai place, with its cheery, lime- and mango-colored
walls, is already showing favor with locals and critics alike. The
chive dumplings, especially, are a standout. Entrées are made with
fresh ingredients and no MSG. They provide water glasses. No
corkage fee.
(773) 467-1168, Mon–Sat 11–9, Sun closed

EN•THAI•CE $
5701 N. Clark (Hollywood), Edgewater
Thai/Vegetarian-Friendly
Dinner specials such as tamarind shrimp and golden shallots
and panang curry with duck and poached lychees, combined
with the simple, cute décor, elevate this 24-seat neighborhood
spot from run-of-the-mill Thai eatery. Owners will cater to
vegans. They provide wine glasses, pint glasses, ice buckets, and
corkscrews. No corkage fee.
(773) 275-3555, www.enthaice.com, Mon closed, Tues–Thurs
11–9, Fri–Sat 11–10, Sun 11–9 🐾

5 LOAVES EATERY $$
2343 E. 71st (Yates), South Shore
American
Named after the Biblical tale of how Jesus fed a crowd of thousands with only five loaves of bread, this eatery will need another divine intervention before they're allowed to serve booze—this district is dry. In the meantime, bring a cold one and feast on po' boys, chicken salad, homemade gumbo, and other comfort food. They provide wine glasses, beer mugs, and corkscrews. No corkage fee. Live jazz the first Friday of the month.
(773) 363-0393, Mon closed, Tues–Thurs 9–7, Fri–Sat 9–8, Sun 9–5 🍴 ♫

FAN SI PAN $
1618 W. Chicago (Ashland), East Ukrainian Village
Pan-Asian/Vietnamese
Susan Furst honed her culinary skills at Four Seasons in Chicago and Flying Fish in Seattle before opening this tiny, bright spot. Regulars love the oversized spring rolls and French-fried beans (which go well with beer, says Furst). For a twist, try gin or vodka with the refreshing honeydew lemonade. They provide plastic cups and corkscrews. No corkage fee.
(773) 738-1405, http://fansipanchicago.com, 11–9 every day

FATTOUSH $$
2652 N. Halsted (Wrightwood), Lincoln Park
Middle Eastern/Vegetarian-Friendly
Named after their signature salad, Fattoush offers authentic Lebanese food in a casual atmosphere in the heart of Lincoln Park. They provide wine glasses, rocks glasses, Champagne buckets, and corkscrews. They will also put your bottles in the fridge and fetch you fresh ones upon request. No corkage fee.
(773) 327-2652, www.fattoushrestaurant.com, Mon–Thurs 11–10, Fri–Sat 11–11, Sun 11–9

FEED $$

2803 W. Chicago (California), Humboldt Park
American

If you find yourself in a neighborhood diner with a plethora of
roosters and a flashing electric Jesus on the walls, you're at Feed.
Owner Donna Knezek, formerly with Leo's Lunchroom and Bite,
serves up chicken (of course), mac-n-cheese, cole slaw, pie, and
other homemade treats. They provide juice and water glasses and
ice buckets. No corkage fee.

(773) 489-4600, Mon–Sat 11–10, Sun closed, cash only 🥢

FIERROS $$$

2550 W. Addison (Rockwell), Lakeview
Argentinian

Fierros serves Argentinian food *tenedor libre* style, which combines elements of buffet and a multi-course meal. Courses are
served one by one, and you can reorder as much as you like—a
great deal for only $15 each. They provide water glasses and ice
buckets and will open bottles. No hard alcohol allowed.

(773) 305-3333, www.fierros-chicago.com, Mon–Tues closed,
Wed–Sat 4:30–10:30, Sun 2–9:30, reservations recommended,
cash only Ⓟ

FLYING SAUCER $$

1123 N. California (Division), Humboldt Park
Eclectic/Vegetarian-Friendly/Brunch

This laid-back, quirky eatery no longer serves dinner, but BYOB
is very welcome at brunch (bring vodka or Champagne to mix
with their freshly squeezed juices). Dishes range from Mexican-
influenced eggs to meatloaf and mashed potatoes to a tofu-
and-rice bowl. They provide rocks glasses and corkscrews. No
corkage fee.

(773) 342-9076, 8–3 every day, cash only

FRIENDSHIP RESTAURANT $$
2830 N. Milwaukee (Diversey), Logan Square
Chinese

For over 25 years, chef and owner Alan Yuen has offered what he calls "180 degrees from ordinary" Chinese cuisine. What emerges is French-inspired upscale Chinese (curry-lime crusted salmon, Peking duck l'orange) in an elegant dining room. They provide Bordeaux wine glasses, beer glasses, and ice buckets, and servers will open bottles. No corkage fee.

(773) 227-0970, www.friendshiprestaurant.com, Mon–Thurs 12–10, Fri–Sat 12–10:30, Sun 3–10, reservations recommended on weekends

GARLIC & CHILI $
1232 N. LaSalle (Division), Old Town
Thai

This restaurant's location—at subterranean level of a transient hotel—is deceiving. Inside is a clean, casual place to enjoy pad Thai, drunken noodle, and a cold Singha, from the same owners of Thai Classic in Lakeview. They provide parfait (beggars can't be choosers) and highball glasses. No corkage fee.

(312) 255-1717, Mon–Sat 11:30–9:30, Sun closed

GINO'S EAST $
2801 N. Lincoln (Diversey), Lakeview
Italian/Pizza

This is still the only Gino's East location that's BYOB—with no plans to obtain a liquor license anytime soon. Enjoy their classic deep dish pizzas, salads, and Italian dinners in a super-casual environment. Beverage service: YOYO. No corkage fee.

(773) 327-3737, www.ginoseast.com, Mon–Thurs 11–10:30, Fri–Sat 11–12, Sun 12–10:30 Ⓟ ⏴

GIO'S CAFÉ & DELI $$
2724 S. Lowe (28th), Bridgeport
Italian

This small Italian grocery-deli, owned by veterans of Rosebud group, attracts Bridgeport neighbors and out-of-towners alike. The few tables here are wedged in between cases of soft drinks and groceries, where diners feast on daily specials such as halibut oreganato and chicken livornese. They provide wine glasses and ice buckets.

(312) 225-6368, www.gioscafe.com, Mon–Sat 10–9, Sun closed

GOLDEN BULL $$

242 W. Cermak (Wentworth), Chinatown
Chinese

If you're hankering for some Mongolian beef after midnight, head down to this eatery, just off the main drag in Chinatown. Very little English is spoken here (the signs in the restaurant are all in Chinese), but the menu is translated to English. Beware the bizarre hours. They provide water glasses. No corkage fee.
(312) 808-1668, 12–4:30p, 9p–2a every day

GRANDE NOODLES & SUSHI BAR $$

6632 N. Clark (Wallen), Rogers Park
Sushi/Thai

With a menu that features over 30 types of maki and dozens of scrumptious Thai selections, this place is bound to please everyone. Because the owner is a police officer, and the city prohibits cops from holding liquor licenses, this place is BYOB indefinitely. They provide wine glasses, pint glasses, ice buckets, and corkscrews. No corkage fee.
(773) 761-6666, www.grandenoodles.com, Mon–Thurs 11:30– 9:30, Fri–Sat 11:30–10, Sun 12–9:30

GREEK CORNER $$

958 N. Damen (Augusta), Ukrainian Village
Greek

For great Greek food outside of Greektown, come to this family-owned place, recently voted "Best Neighborhood Joint" in the Ukrainian Village area by *Chicago* magazine. Homemade moussaka, "Greek Pizza," daily specials, and lamb shank (Fridays only) top the favorites list. They provide wine glasses and will open your bottles.
(773) 252-8010, Mon–Sat 11:30–10, Sun closed 🦅

HB $$$
3403 N. Halsted (Roscoe), Lakeview
Contemporary American/Brunch

Formerly a storefront for their catering business, the restaurant-formerly-known-as-The-Hearty-Boys has remodeled and expanded their charming dining room to seat 42. Chef Joncarl Lachman selects the finest in organic, locally grown produce and whips up unique twists on traditional American fare. The results? Fabulous seafood entrées, tasty salads, and traditional favorites such as chops, steaks, and chicken—all served with TLC by the attentive waitstaff. Bloody Marys are popular at brunch, and there are plenty of sodas and freshly squeezed juices to mix with spirits. Call for more information on dinner specials, special events, and the weekly prix fixe menu. They provide wine glasses, pint glasses, martini glasses, martini shakers, limes, Bloody Mary mix, and celery rim salt. Customers even bring their own martini shakers and stir or shake their own. No corkage fee.

(773) 244-9866, www.heartyboys.com, Mon closed, Tues–Sat 5–10, Sun 4–9 (dinner), Sat–Sun 9–2 (brunch)

HAMA MATSU $$$
5143 N. Clark (Foster), Andersonville
Sushi/Japanese/Korean

With superstars Sushi Luxe and Tanoshii down the street, it's getting harder to justify this option for sushi. However, BYOB is popular here. They provide wine glasses, sake cups, martini glasses, Champagne flutes, and corkscrews.

(773) 506-2978, www.hamamatsu-restaurant.com, Mon–Fri 3–11, Sat 12–11, Sun 12–1

HASHALOM RESTAURANT $
2905 W. Devon (Francisco), West Rogers Park
Israeli/Moroccan

You can't go wrong with anything on the menu at this cute, casual neighborhood place, especially the Moroccan couscous, which is served only on Friday and Saturday nights. Beverage service: YOYO. No corkage fee.

(773) 465-5675, Mon–Tues closed, Wed–Sun 12–9

HEALTHY FOOD LITHUANIAN RESTAURANT $$
3236 S. Halsted (32nd), Bridgeport
Lithuanian/American

When owner Gina Biciunas-Santoski's parents bought this restaurant in 1960 (it originally opened in 1938), there were at least half a dozen Lithuanian restaurants in this area. Today, Healthy Food Lithuanian is the only one left standing. This is a restaurant not just worth eating at, it's a slice of Chicago history. You are urged to make the trip to see this "frozen-in-time" diner, with its comfy booths, counter seating, and Naugahyde-covered chairs. Read the story on the wall about how this place got its "Healthy" name. Feast on the authentic, stick-to-your-ribs Lithuanian food based on recipes older than the diner itself. There are authentic *kugelis* (made with potatoes, eggs, onions, and bacon, and served with sour cream), *koldunai* (boiled meat dumplings), cheese dumplings, stuffed cabbage, cold beet soup, and the popular *blynai* (Lithuanian pancakes topped with fresh blueberries, cranberries, apples, and other fruit in season). There are also several American dishes (grilled pork chops, grilled fish) to enjoy. Soak in the atmosphere. Buy one of the pieces of amber jewelry for sale at the counter or a "kugelis is the breakfast of champions" sweatshirt. And above all, meet Gina Biciunas-Santoski. She is gracious and comforting as a candle in the window. She will urge you to relax, sit down, and you will probably eat until you can eat no more. She will also provide wine glasses, beer glasses, and corkscrews. No corkage fee.

(312) 326-2724, Mon closed, Tues–Wed 7–4, Thurs–Sat 7–8, Sun 8–5, cash only ATM

HEMA'S KITCHEN $$
6406 N. Oakley (Devon), West Rogers Park
Indian/Vegetarian-Friendly

Both locations serve homemade Northern and Southern Indian food. They don't take reservations, so there can be a wait, especially on the weekends. There are liquor stores near both locations that sell several types of Indian beer if you're caught empty-handed. They provide wine glasses and corkscrews and will put your bottles in the fridge. No corkage fee.

(773) 338-1627, www.hemaskitchen.net, 12–11 every day

HEMA'S KITCHEN II $$
2411 N. Clark (Fullerton), Lincoln Park
Indian/Vegetarian-Friendly
(773) 529-1705, www.hemaskitchen.net, 12–11 every day

HOANG THANH $$
1129 W. Argyle (Broadway), Uptown
Vietnamese
Hoang Thanh features nearly 300 menu items in an atmosphere that's several notches above the casual noodle shops on this strip of Argyle. If you forgo BYOB, there are delicious bubble teas made from fresh mangos, avocados, coconuts, and more (think "Jamba Juice" of Argyle Street). They provide wine glasses and corkscrews. No corkage fee.
(773) 271-7328, Wed–Mon 11–10, Tues closed

HOT DOUG'S $
3324 N. California (Roscoe), Irving Park
Eclectic
Hot Doug's takes premium sausages, tops them with gourmet ingredients, then names these "dogs" after pop celebrities. Will it be the "Elvis," a smoked polish, or the "Bobby Douglass," a smoked shrimp and pork sausage with Creole mustard tartar and bleu cheese? Duck fat fries are served on Fridays and Saturdays. They have plastic cups on hand. No corkage fee.
(773) 279-9550, www.hotdougs.com, Mon–Sat 10:30–4, Sun closed

INDIAN GRILL $$
2258 N. Clark (Webster), Lincoln Park
Indian
This place had a liquor license, but the owners gave it up due to the "hassles" involved. Décor is slightly upscale yet inviting, with white linen tablecloths and gorgeous photography of India on the walls. They provide wine glasses and corkscrews and will open bottles and put them in the cooler. No corkage fee.
(773) 477-8000, www.indiangrillrestaurant.com, Mon–Tues 5–10, Wed–Thurs 11:30–3, 5–10, Fri–Sat 11:30–3, 5–11, Sun 11:30–3, 5–10

INDIE CAFÉ $$$
5951 N. Broadway (Thorndale), Rogers Park
Sushi/Japanese/Thai

"Café" is misleading; this is a contemporary, critically praised sushi bar that serves up equally good Japanese and Thai cuisines. They may obtain their liquor license in the future but will accommodate BYOB customers either way. They provide wine glasses, pilsner glasses, sake cups, and corkscrews and will put your bottles in the cooler. No corkage fee.

(773) 561-5577, www.indiecafe.us, Mon–Thurs 11:30–10, Fri–Sat 11:30–10:30, Sun 12–10

IRAZU $$
1865 N. Milwaukee (Oakley), Wicker Park
Costa Rican

Aptly named after a Costa Rican volcano, this neighborhood gem is almost always bursting at the seams with customers. Dive into the fried plantains, combination plate, or daily dinner specials for a unique dining experience. They provide plastic cups and will chill your bottles upon request. No corkage fee.

(773) 252-5687, Mon–Sat 11–9, Sun closed, cash only Ⓟ 🎏

JAI-YEN FUSION RESTAURANT $$
3736 N. Broadway (Grace), Lakeview
Sushi/Thai

Jai-yen is Thai for "be patient; relax," which is exactly the vibe called for at this cute space, formerly occupied by Genesee Depot. One of the owners was a sushi chef at both Sushi Samba and Tsunami. They provide red and white wine stemware, pilsner glasses, sake cups, and ice buckets. They will also heat up your sake in the microwave upon request and open your bottles as soon as you're seated. No corkage fee.

(773) 404-0555, www.jai-yen.com, Sun–Thurs 11:30–10:30, Fri–Sat 11:30–11

JAMAICA GATES RESTAURANT $$
618 Church (Chicago), Evanston
Jamaican

Find jerk chicken, curry goat, brown stew snapper, and nightly specials at this small, bright, family-run joint in downtown Evanston. They provide wine glasses, pint glasses, and corkscrews and will put your bottles in the cooler upon request. No corkage fee.
(847) 869-1629, Mon–Sat 11:30–10, Sun 12–8

JAPONICA $$$
1422 W. Taylor (Loomis), University Village/Little Italy
Sushi/Japanese

If you're looking to cure your sushi fix in this area of mostly Italian restaurants, Japonica will hit the spot (and it's permanently BYOB). Sushi chefs here have decades of experience. They provide you with bistro-style glasses and corkscrews. No corkage fee.
(312) 421-3288, www.dinejaponica.com, Mon–Thurs 11:30–10, Fri 11:30–11, Sat 4–11, Sun closed

JASMINE RICE $
3103 N. Narragansett (Belmont), Belmont Central
Thai

This cozy eatery (formerly Red Ginger) in a residential area is tastefully decorated with hand-painted lithos and décor shipped over from Thailand for a charming yet contemporary feel. The curries and "chef's specials" are favorites here. They provide wine glasses, beer glasses, and ice buckets and will open bottles. No corkage fee.
(773) 836-1288, Mon closed, Tues–Sat 11–10, Sun 11:30–10

JIM NOODLE & RICE $
2819 N. Lincoln (Diversey), Lakeview
Thai/Vegetarian-Friendly

If there were a "smallest BYOB" award, this place would win hands down. The dining room only seats 12 next to an open grill, but in the summer an outdoor garden patio accommodates 16. Vegetarians can choose from almost 30 entrées. Beverage service: YOYO. No corkage fee.
(773) 935-5923, Mon–Sat 11:30–10, Sun 12–10

JITLADA THAI HOUSE $

3715 N. Halsted (Grace), Lakeview
Thai

This neighborhood spot recently expanded to twice its size, but so far owners do not have plans to apply for a liquor license. The menu features traditional Thai appetizers, soups, noodle and rice dishes, and entrées. They provide water glasses and corkscrews. No corkage fee.

(773) 388-9988, www.jitladathaihouse.com, 11:30–11:30 every day Ⓟ 🔺

JOY'S NOODLES & RICE $

3257 N. Broadway (Belmont), Lakeview
Thai

This Lakeview favorite is almost always packed at any time of the day or night. They serve all the traditional Thai favorites—pad Thai, satay, tom kha—along with curries and rice dishes. They provide wine glasses. No corkage fee.

(773) 327-8330, Sun–Thurs 11–10, Fri–Sat 11–11 🔺

JOY YEE NOODLE $$

521 Davis (Chicago), Evanston
Pan-Asian

All three city locations are popular, bustling hives of activity, and all are BYOB. The menu contains separate Thai, Korean, Chinese, and Vietnamese dishes, rather than a blend of all four cuisines. If you can't decide what to order, the "food art" in the window may help you choose. They provide water glasses and corkscrews. No corkage fee.

(847) 733-1900, www.joyyee.com, Mon–Thurs 11:30–9, Fri–Sat 11:30–10, Sun 12–9 🔺

JOY YEE NOODLE $$

2159 S. China Place (Cermak), Chinatown
Pan-Asian

If you find the surrounding authentic Chinese restaurants out of your comfort zone, Joy Yee provides a slightly more Anglo-friendly option. This location, in the Chinatown Square, also features a walk-up window, at which you can order a de-lish fresh-fruit bubble tea or "freeze" (if you can decide among the dozens of tempting choices). They provide water glasses and corkscrews. No corkage fee.

(312) 328-0001, ww.joyyee.com, 11–10:30 every day

JOY YEE NOODLE $$

1335 S. Halsted (13th), University Village
Pan-Asian

(312) 997-2128, www.joyyee.com, Mon–Thurs 11:30–9, Fri–Sat 11:30–10, Sun 12–9

J-THAI SUSHI BAR AND THAI CUISINE $$

3819–21 N. Southport (Grace), Lakeview
Sushi/Thai

Open since fall 2005 in the space formerly occupied by Banana Leaf, J-Thai offers reasonably priced food on an increasingly hip strip of Southport. The sushi chef here hails from Sushi Wabi. They provide wine glasses, ice buckets, and corkscrews and servers will open bottles upon request (no sake cups; "The sake bombers broke them all!"). No corkage fee.

(773) 883-8683, www.j-thai.com, Mon–Thurs 4–10:30, Fri–Sun 11–11

KABUL HOUSE $$

3220 Dempster (McCormick), Evanston
Afghan

Authentic Afghan décor, music, and cuisine all draw you in for a truly unique experience. The private alcoves make for an intimate dining experience. They provide wine glasses, ice buckets, and corkscrews. They will open bottles or put them in the cooler upon request.

(847) 763-9930, www.kabulhouse.com, Mon closed, Tues–Sat 11:30–10, Sun 1–9, reservations recommended on weekends P

KAN ZAMAN $$$
617 N. Wells (Ohio), River North
Middle Eastern
Kan Zaman's ("once upon a time" in Arabic) simple, tasteful décor
and traditional Lebanese seating provide a beautiful backdrop for
the mouth-watering cuisine and excellent service, which begins
the moment you walk in. It's a perfect place for special occasions.
They provide red wine glasses, chilled white wine glasses, chilled
Champagne flutes, chilled beer mugs, rocks glasses, cordial and
shooter glasses, Champagne buckets, and servers will automati-
cally open your wine and chill your bottles.
(312) 751-9600, Mon–Thurs 11–10, Fri–Sat 11–12, Sun 1–10,
reservations recommended 🥡 ♫

KARYN'S $$
1901 N. Halsted (Armitage), Lincoln Park
Vegetarian-Friendly/Brunch
Karyn Calabrese offers raw, organic, vegan cuisine in an elegant
dining room, complete with white linen tablecloths and contemporary décor. Entrées include the tempting basil ravioli with
macadamia whipped crème and sun-dried tomato puree. They
provide wine glasses, Champagne flutes, martini glasses, and
corkscrews.
(312) 255-1590, www.karynraw.com, 11:30–10 every day, Sun
brunch 11:30–3:30 Ⓟ 🥡

KATACHI $$
3911 N. Sheridan (Irving Park), Lakeview
Sushi/Japanese
This cute, contemporary spot in Lakeview features a full sushi
bar, a maki menu for vegetarians, and an unbelievable $19.95 all-
you-can-eat sushi special from 5–7 after Cubs' home games. They
provide pilsner glasses, sake cups, sake pitchers, and ice buckets
and will heat up your sake in the microwave.
(773) 880-5340, www.katachisushi.com, Sun–Thurs 5–10,
Fri–Sat 5–11 🥡

KIKUYA $$$
1601 E. 55th (Lake Park), Hyde Park
Japanese/Sushi
Remember traditional sushi? Fresh fish presented simply on a bed
of sushi rice, instead of piled high with a kitchen sink of ingredients? Kikuya offers authentic, classic sushi and made-from-scratch
Japanese cuisine near the University of Chicago. They provide
wine glasses, beer mugs, sake cups, sake pitchers, and ice buckets
and will warm up your sake in boiling water. No corkage fee.
(773) 667-3727, www.kikuyaonline.com, Mon closed, Tues–Sun
12–9:30, reservations recommended on weekends (while school is
in session)

KOKEERI RESTAURANT $
4346 W. Lawrence (Kostner), Mayfair
Korean
This spacious, bright place specializes in Korean noodle dishes
and homemade mandoo (dumplings filled with meat and
vegetable combinations). Everything is prepared as spicy as you
can handle (mostly "locals" eat here). Private party room in front
seats up to 32. Beverage service: YOYO (we asked for a corkscrew
and were given a can opener). No corkage fee.
(773) 205-5680, Mon–Sat 10–10, Sun closed

LA CAZUELA MARISCOS $$$
6922 N. Clark (Morse), Rogers Park
Mexican
This sun-filled eatery specializes in Mexican seafood. Dishes
include mussels in garlic and wine sauce and red snapper with
onions, tomatoes, and wine sauce. Free parking at First Commer-
cial Bank (at the corner) after 6 on weekdays, after 3 on Saturday,
and all day Sunday. They provide wine glasses, beer glasses, ice
buckets, and corkscrews. No corkage fee.
(773) 338-5425, Mon–Thurs 10–10, Fri–Sat 10–11, Sun 9–11 Ⓟ ⚑

LA COCINA DE GALARZA RESTAURANT $$
2420 W. Fullerton (Western), Logan Square
Puerto Rican

This friendly, family-run restaurant has served homemade Puerto Rican food in the neighborhood since 1990. The dining room is small, but the inviting outdoor patio in back is a well-kept secret for private parties. Their virgin piña coladas are a perfect excuse to break out the rum. They provide wine glasses.

(773) 235-7377, Mon–Thurs 12–9, Fri–Sat 12–10, Sun 12–9 ⛺

LA CUCINA DI DONATELLA $$$
2221 W. Howard (Bell), West Rogers Park
Italian

Italian chef/owner Donatella provides simple, fresh, Italian cuisine in a light, airy dining room that features blond hardwood and white linen tablecloths. There are daily seafood, pasta, and meat specials, plus decadent desserts and thin-crust Italian pizza. They provide white and red wine stemware, Champagne flutes, and ice buckets; servers will open bottles.

(773) 262-6533, Sun–Thurs 5:30–9, Fri–Sat 5:30–10, reservations recommended on weekends Ⓟ ⛺

LA SIERRA $$
1637 W. Montrose (Ashland), Ravenswood
Mexican/Ecuadorian

La Sierra features both Mexican and Ecuadorian cuisines. For beginners, *llampingachos* and *seco de chivo* (goat stew cooked in beer) are two good introductions to the latter. Customers are allowed to bring their own tequila, margarita mix, and margarita glasses. They provide wine glasses and ice buckets. No corkage fee.

(773) 549-5538, 10–10 every day

LINCOLN PARK'S NOODLE HOUSE $$
2428 N. Ashland (Fullerton), Lincoln Park
Thai/Japanese/Sushi

Deceiving from the outside, Lincoln Park's Noodle House features a long, narrow dining room that seats 100, with a private party and karaoke room for 35 in back. The atmosphere is contemporary, almost clubby. Bring stemware for parties of 10 or more. They provide some wine glasses and corkscrews. No corkage fee.

(773) 248-6680, www.lincolnparksnoodles.com, Mon closed, Tues–Thurs 11–10:30, Fri–Sat 11–11, Sun 4–10:30

LOS NOPALES $$
4544 N. Western (Wilson), Lincoln Square
Mexican/Brunch
Grilled skirt steak is a highlight at this promising new Mexican spot, especially when served over *frijoles borrachos* (drunken beans) with cactus salad. I dare you to skip the velvety, rich flan in coffee, almond, chocolate, coconut, orange, or vanilla. The party room in back seats 50. They provide wine glasses, pilsner glasses, ice buckets, and corkscrews. No corkage fee.
(773) 334-3149, Mon closed, Tues–Sun 10–10

LUC THANG $
1524 N. Ashland (North), Wicker Park
Thai/Chinese/Vietnamese
Since 1997, this small storefront has served Thai, Vietnamese, and Chinese food to neighborhood regulars. For the uninitiated, popular Vietnamese dishes are the Vietnamese *com suon* and Vietnamese grilled beef noodle. Or, on the Thai side, the panang with sweet curry is highly rated. They provide wine glasses and have an ice bucket on hand (yes, there's only one). No corkage fee.
(773) 395-3907, Sun–Thurs 11–10, Fri–Sat 11–11

LUCIA RISTORANTE $$$
1825 W. North (Honore), Wicker Park
Italian
If you just walk by Lucia's storefront deli, you'll miss the fine dining room tucked away in back. This light, airy, elegant space seats 54, while the outdoor patio seats 30 in the summer. Critics and customers rave about the authentic Italian menu, which includes homemade pastas, seafood entrées, antipasti, salads, and homemade desserts. A true neighborhood gem. They provide white and red wine glasses, imported Italian Champagne flutes, beer glasses, and ice buckets, and servers will open bottles. No corkage fee.
(773) 292-9700, Mon–Thurs 5–10, Fri–Sat 5–11, Sun 4–9,
reservations recommended every night 🐾

M. HENRY $$
5707 N. Clark (Hollywood), Edgewater
Contemporary American/Brunch

This exquisite breakfast and lunch spot is becoming the Bongo
Room of the far north side. Creative egg dishes, sandwiches, and
French toast, all on artisan breads, tempt the palate. Customers
can bring in Bloody Mary mix and vodka. They provide wine
stemware, bistro-style glasses, Champagne flutes, and ice buckets,
and servers will open bottles. No corkage fee.
(773) 561-1600, www.mhenry.net, Tues–Fri 7–2:30, Sat–Sun 8–3,
reservations recommended

MR. THAI $
3811 N. Ashland (Grace), Lakeview
Thai

It's a little tough parking around here, but once inside you'll find an
extensive menu of traditional Thai cuisine, like moo ping (grilled
skewered pork) and pad khee mao. They provide wine glasses,
pilsner glasses, corkscrews, and ice buckets. No corkage fee.
(773) 244-9300, Mon–Fri 11:30–10, Sat–Sun 12–10

MAMACITA'S $$
2439 N. Clark (Fullerton), Lincoln Park
Mexican/Vegetarian-Friendly/Brunch

Mamacita's in Lincoln Park—the only location left—offers a
modern spin on Mexican cuisine. The menu includes mushroom
and poblano pizza and nachos with goat cheese. Breakfast is
served until 3 every day. They provide plastic cups, corkscrews,
and limes and will put your bottles in the fridge upon request. No
corkage fee.
(773) 404-7788, www.mamacitarestaurant.com, Mon–Sat 10–10,
Sun 9–9

MANDARIN KITCHEN $$
2143 S. Archer (Cermak), Chinatown
Chinese

"Hot pots" are the specialty at this cute, spacious place. Dim sum,
sizzling rice, beaucoup seafood dishes, and an abundance of noodle
soups are also available, plus several "American favorites" for more
mainstream tastes. They provide water glasses. No corkage fee.
(312) 328-0228, Mon 11–10:30, Tues 3–10:30, Wed–Thurs
11–10:30, Fri–Sun 9–11

MARK'S CHOP SUEY $
3343 N. Halsted (Buckingham), Lakeview
Chinese
Mark's has been serving Lakeview locals traditional, consistently
good Chinese food (the cashew chicken is to-die) for over 30
years. Not too many people BYOB here—it's mainly a place to
grab a bite before heading to the myriad bars in the area—but
it is welcome. They provide water glasses and corkscrews. No
corkage fee.
(773) 281-9090, Mon closed, Tues–Sun 3–11

MARRAKECH CUISINE $$
1413 N. Ashland (Blackhawk), Noble Square
Moroccan/Mediterranean
This unassuming storefront belies a charming restaurant that
serves an ever-changing menu of delicious Moroccan food. On
weekends, belly dancers and live North African and Middle
Eastern music liven up the place. They provide wine glasses, beer
mugs, Champagne flutes, and ice buckets.
(773) 227-6451, www.marrakechcuisin.com, Mon closed,
Tues–Sun 5–11, reservations recommended on weekends ♫

MATSU YAMA $$$
1059 W. Belmont (Seminary), Lakeview
Japanese/Sushi
Matsu Yama features contemporary, slightly upscale ambience in
a dining room that seats almost 100 (including about 10 at the
sushi bar). They offer a full maki, sushi, and sashimi menu, plus
several grilled options for the sushi-shy. They have wine glasses,
Champagne flutes, sake cups, and ice buckets on hand, and will
warm up your sake in the microwave. No corkage fee.
(773) 327-8838, www.matsuyamasushi.com, Mon–Tues 5–11,
Wed–Thurs 11–2:30, 4:30–11; Fri–Sat 11:30–2:30, 5–12;
Sun 5–10, reservations recommended on weekends

MAY ST. CAFÉ $$$
1146 W. Cermak (May), Pilsen
Nuevo Latino/Eclectic

Chef Mario Santiago features Mexican, Puerto Rican, Cuban, and
American cuisine—all with a contemporary twist—at this beautiful but out-of-the-way eatery. Start things off with an appetizer
such as the French double cream brie and pear quesadillas, then
move on to entrées such as salmon with tequila lemon butter
chipotle cream sauce and rice and beans. Dessert options include
mango flan and sweet plantain soufflé in phyllo. (Is your mouth
watering yet?) They provide bistro-style glasses and pilsner glasses
and servers will open your bottles.

(312) 421-4442, www.maystcafe.com, Mon closed, Tues–Thurs
5–10, Fri–Sat 5–11, Sun 5–9, reservations recommended
every night Ⓟ

MEDICI ON 57TH $
1327 E. 57th (Kenwood), Hyde Park
American/Brunch

The eclectic menu caters to standard (chicken wings, ravioli) and
adventuresome (Moroccan ragout, baked goat cheese) tastes. The
booths and walls at this funky loft are heavily engraved with diners' names and quotes—even a few math problems. They provide
rocks glasses and corkscrews; only wine and beer allowed. No
corkage fee.

(773) 667-7394, www.medici57.com, Mon–Thurs 12–11:30, Fri
11–12, Sat 9–12:30, Sun 9–11 🦅

MEI SHUNG $$
5511 N. Broadway (Catalpa), Edgewater
Taiwanese/Chinese

This is one of the city's only authentic Taiwanese restaurants, with
more seafood entrées than you can count. Dining is family-style,
which allows customers to share and sample several different
dishes. There's limited free parking in the church lot across the
street. They provide wine glasses and ice buckets and will open
your bottles upon request. No corkage fee.

(773) 728-5778, www.meishung.com, Mon closed,
Tues–Fri 11:30–10, Sat 12–11, Sun 12–9:30, reservations
recommended Ⓟ

MYSORE WOODLANDS $$
2548 W. Devon (Rockwell), West Rogers Park
Indian/Vegetarian-Friendly
Serving vegetarian-only Southern Indian cuisine, Mysore Woodlands has been a mainstay on this strip of Indian restaurants for
nearly 10 years. They provide water glasses and corkscrews. No
corkage fee charged for 1–4 people.
(773) 338-8160, Sun–Thurs 11:30–9:30, Fri–Sat 11–10 Ⓟ

NAN'S SUSHI & CHINESE $$
2360 N. Lincoln (Fullerton), Lincoln Park
Chinese/Sushi
Next to Nan's busy takeout storefront is a separate dining room,
which features slightly lavish Asian décor and a sushi bar. The
enormous pot stickers are a meal all by themselves. Free parking
after 5 in Children's Memorial garage. They provide wine glasses,
sake cups, and ice buckets. Servers will open wine bottles or
provide corkscrews upon request. No corkage fee.
(773) 935-5900, www.urbaneateries.com/nans, Sun–Thurs
11:30–10, Fri–Sat 11:30–11 Ⓟ

NEW JEANNY'S RESTAURANT $$
1053 W. Belmont (Seminary), Lakeview
Chinese
Most of the business here is delivery, but New Jeanny's also has a
full-sized dining room. Dinner specials are priced around $9 and
include soup and appetizer. There's an odd assortment of cordial,
margarita, Champagne, and other glasses left by the previous
owners. They also provide corkscrews. No corkage fee.
(773) 248-1133, www.newjeannys.com, Mon–Thurs 11:30–10,
Fri–Sat 11:30–10:30, Sun 12–10

NEW TOKYO $$$
3139 N. Broadway (Briar), Lakeview
Sushi/Japanese
For over 10 years, this neighborhood place has served some of
the best (yes, I said best) sushi in the city. Owner Sung Kim flies
in fresh, high-quality fish daily and also cooks the most delicious
traditional Japanese cuisine. Beverage service is spotty, but hey, no
corkage. They provide juice glasses, pint glasses, ice buckets, and
corkscrews—all upon request. No corkage fee.
(773) 248-1193, Mon–Fri 2–11, Sat–Sun 12–11 ⟋

NHU HOA CAFÉ $$

1020 W. Argyle (Sheridan), Uptown
Vietnamese/Laotian

This is a more formal dining option along a strip of casual noodle shops. The clay pots and lemongrass chicken are definitely worth the trip, and there's a party room for up to 40 in the back. They provide wine glasses, Champagne glasses and flutes, and corkscrews. No corkage fee.

(773) 878-0618, www.nhuhoacafe.bizland.com, Mon closed, Tues–Thurs 10–10, Fri–Sat 10–10:30, Sun 10–10

NILE RESTAURANT $$

1611 E. 55th (Cornell), Hyde Park
Middle Eastern

This place serves up incredible shish kabobs. The secret is in the cuts of meat—only lamb from the loin and filet mignon will do. Several delicious seafood, lamb, veggie, beef, and chicken entrées are also available. They provide rocks glasses (but they're used for tea and coffee, so you may want to bring your own glassware) and corkscrews. No hard liquor allowed. No corkage fee.

(773) 324-9499, Mon–Sat 11–9, Sun 12–8

THE NOODLE $

2336 S. Wentworth (23rd), Chinatown
Vietnamese

Curiously located in the heart of Chinatown is this cute Vietnamese spot serving (hmm...what could it be?) noodles. The menu is split into two parts: "for beginners" offerings include classic pho and vermicelli dishes; the "adventurer's choice" explores tripe, tendon, and other cuts of meat. Beverage service: YOYO. No corkage fee.

(312) 674-1168, 10–10 every day

NOODLES ETC. $
1460 E. 53rd (Harper), Hyde Park
Pan-Asian
Two locations serve up pan-Asian stir-fry in open-kitchen style
(think Penny's Noodle, Zen's). This location has a lofted space
for small parties. Their Web site boasts "light FM played in
background," so I was amused to hear Def Leppard blasting on
a recent visit. They provide corkscrews and, curiously, some
Champagne flutes behind the cash register. No corkage fee.
(773) 947-8787, www.noodlesetc.com, Mon–Sat 11–10,
Sun 11:30–9:30

NOODLES ETC. $
1333 E. 57th (Kenwood), Hyde Park
Pan-Asian
This second location—next to the University of Chicago cam-
pus—also features affordable Thai, Vietnamese, Japanese, and
Chinese dishes. The décor here is more updated than the other
location. Beverage service: YOYO. No corkage fee.
(773) 684-2807, www.noodlesetc.com, Mon–Sat 11–10,
Sun 11:30–9:30

NOODLE ZONE $
5427 N. Clark (Rascher), Andersonville
Thai/Sushi
Owners recently expanded this space, added a sushi bar, and gave
everything a nice, bright, contemporary look. They provide wine
glasses, beer mugs, ice buckets, and corkscrews. No corkage fee.
(773) 293-1089, www.noodlezone.net, Mon–Thurs 11:30–9:30,
Fri–Sat 11:30–10, Sun 12–9:30

NOODLES IN THE POT $
2453 N. Halsted (Fullerton), Lincoln Park
Thai
The owners of this cute spot in the DePaul area also own Joy's on
Broadway. They used to have a liquor license but gave it up ("too
much hassle"). Enjoy the new BYOB policy and the charming
outdoor patio in the summertime. They provide wine glasses,
pilsner glasses, and corkscrews. No corkage fee.
(773) 975-6177, Sun–Thurs 11–10, Fri–Sat 11–11 ⬈

NOOKIES TREE $$$

3334 N. Halsted (Buckingham), Lakeview
American/Brunch

Nookies has always been a popular breakfast spot, but their dinner menu has evolved recently to include such inventive entrées as cider-marinated grilled pork chops and maplewood-smoked chicken. They also offer steaks, seafood, pasta, comfort food, and breakfast all day. They provide wine glasses (there's OJ for mimosas) and ice buckets, and servers will open bottles upon request. An assortment of mixers such as Bloody Mary mix is in the works. No corkage fee.

(773) 248-9888, www.nookiesrestaurants.com, Sun–Thurs 7a–midnight, Fri–Sat 24 hrs., cash only 🥢 ATM

NOOKIES $$$

1746 N. Wells (Eugenie), Old Town
American/Brunch

This original Nookies location has served breakfast to the Old Town neighborhood since 1973—and now serves lunch and dinner. They provide wine glasses and ice buckets, and servers will open bottles upon request. No corkage fee.

(312) 337-2454, www.nookiesrestaurants.com, Mon–Sat 6:30a–10p, Sun 6:30a–9p, cash only 🥢 ATM

NOOKIES TOO $$$

2114 N. Halsted (Dickens), Lincoln Park
American/Brunch

This is a perfect place to relax and dig into a hot, hearty meal after a shop-til-you-drop afternoon on Armitage or Halsted. Or, indulge in a few Bloody Marys at a late brunch on the weekend. They provide wine glasses and ice buckets, and servers will open bottles upon request. No corkage fee.

(773) 327-1400, www.nookiesrestaurants.com, Sun–Thurs 7a–3:30p, Fri–Sat 24 hrs.

NORTH COAST CAFÉ $$$
3613 N. Broadway (Addison), Lakeview
American/Brunch
This busy, charming spot is popular with locals for its reliably
good, Greek-influenced menu and weekend brunch. Free parking
at North Community Bank after 5 on weekdays, after 3 on
Saturday, and all day Sunday. Bloody Mary mix and vodka are
allowed, as is Champagne. They provide wine glasses and beer
mugs. No corkage fee.
(773) 549-7606, Mon–Sat 7–10, Sun 7–9 Ⓟ 🔺

NUEVO LÉON RESTAURANT $$
1515 W. 18th (Ashland), Pilsen
Mexican
This family-run restaurant has been a landmark in the heart of
Pilsen since 1962 and is named after their native land, Nuevo
Léon, Mexico. The dinner highlights are ribeye steak, fajitas, and
filete Nuévo Leon (NY strip steak served with rice, beans, potatoes,
and guacamole). They provide water glasses, ice buckets, and
corkscrews. No corkage fee.
(312) 421-1517, www.nuevoleonrestaurant.com, Mon–Sat
7a–midnight, Sun 7a–11p, cash only

OLD JERUSALEM RESTAURANT $$
1411 N. Wells (Schiller), Old Town
Middle Eastern/Vegetarian-Friendly
Old Jerusalem has served consistent, delicious, made-to-order
Lebanese food on beautiful Wells St. in Old Town since 1976. Try
the mouth-watering shawerma sandwiches—thick slices of lamb
or beef piled into a pita with onions, tomatoes, lettuce, and tahini
sauce. They provide wine glasses, pint glasses, and corkscrews.
(312) 944-0459, www.oldjerusalemrestaurant.com, 11–11
every day 🔺

OLIVE MOUNTAIN $$
610 Davis (Chicago), Evanston
Mediterranean

For over 16 years, Olive Mountain has served Evanston residents and visitors an extensive menu of Mediterranean mainstays (shish kabobs, shawerma) as well as unique offerings (Mediterranean pizza). They provide rocks glasses, ice buckets, and corkscrews. No corkage fee.
(847) 475-0380, www.olivemountainrestaurant.com, Mon–Fri 11–9 (closed from 3–5), Sat 5–10, Sun 5–8:30

OODLES OF NOODLES $
2540 N. Clark (Wrightwood), Lincoln Park
Pan-Asian

As the name implies, there are dozens of different noodle dishes available here, from Japanese udon soup to pad Thai to crispy Cantonese noodles. They provide wine glasses, Champagne flutes, and ice buckets, and servers will open bottles. No corkage fee.
(773) 975-1090, www.onoodles.com, Mon–Thurs 11–10, Fri–Sat 11–10:30, Sun 11:30–10

OPART THAI HOUSE $
4658 N. Western (Wilson), Lincoln Square
Thai

Finally open again after an extensive remodeling project, Opart Thai House is now double in size. And they are staying BYOB, despite previous plans to the contrary. They provide wine glasses. No corkage fee.
(773) 989-8517, www.opartthai.com, Sun–Thurs 11–10, Fri–Sat 11–11

ORANGE $$$
3231 N. Clark (Belmont), Lakeview
Brunch/Contemporary American/Eclectic

Known for its eclectic brunch menu, this location now serves dinner. Most entrées are for meat lovers—roasted rack of lamb, braised pork shank, and London broil, to name a few. They provide red and white wine stemware and corkscrews. No corkage fee.
(773) 549-4400, www.orangebrunch.com, Mon–Thurs 9–2, 6–11, Fri 8–2, 5–10, Sat–Sun 8–3, 5–10 🐾

ORANGE $$

75 W. Harrison (Clark), South Loop
Brunch/Eclectic

BYOB is more popular at this location, especially during weekend brunch. The green eggs and ham (scrambled eggs with basil pesto, roasted tomatoes, buffalo mozzarella) and other unique egg and French toast dishes are a huge draw. Discounted garage parking next door. They provide water glasses and corkscrews. No corkage fee.

(312) 447-1000, www.orangebrunch.com, Mon–Fri 8–2, Sat–Sun 8–3

OVER EASY CAFÉ $

4943 N. Damen (Argyle), Ravenswood
American/Brunch

Over Easy Café was recovering from a fire last time I looked, with plans to rebuild. Hopefully this bright breakfast and lunch BYOB will continue to offer their creative egg dishes, especially the "sassy eggs"—two eggs served over chorizo-potato hash with cheddar, red pepper, jalapenos, garlic, sour cream, and ancho chili ketchup.

(773) 506-2605, Mon closed, Tues–Sun 7–3

P.S. BANGKOK 2 $

2521 N. Halsted (Wrightwood), Lincoln Park
Thai

Open since 1985, this is literally P.S. Bangkok in Lakeview's "sister" location. Standout dishes include the panang chicken and pad Thai. They provide wine glasses, corkscrews, and ice buckets or tubs of ice ("People bring in lots of beer here!"). No corkage fee.

(773) 348-0072, www.psbangkok2.com, Mon–Thurs 11–10, Fri–Sat 11:30–11, Sun 4:30–10

PALMITO'S $$$

3605 N. Ashland (Addison), Lakeview
Costa Rican

This is a promising new BYOB that serves Costa Rican cuisine with a contemporary spin (think tilapia ceviche and chicken with shallot-rosemary-mango sauce). They provide wine glasses, beer glasses, and ice buckets, and servers open bottles upon request.

(773) 248-3087, Mon closed, Tues–Fri 5–10, Sat–Sun 11–3, 5–10

PANANG $

800 N. Clark (Chicago), **Near North**
Thai

If you've done some damage to your credit cards in nearby Gold Coast, here's a chance to redeem yourself and save some cash by going BYOB. There are many fine wine stores in the area (and a liquor store across the street that will do "in a pinch"). They provide wine and pilsner glasses. No corkage.
(312) 573-9999, www.panangthai.com, Sun–Thurs 11–9:30, Fri–Sat 11–10:30 🐦

PAPACITO'S MEXICAN GRILLE $

2960 N. Lincoln (Wellington), **Lakeview**
Mexican/Brunch

This new spot on Lincoln, owned by the same family that owns Mamacita's (Little Mama, Little Papa—get it?), serves Mexican comfort food with a few unique twists, such as mango and peach pancakes for brunch and marinated, grilled tilapia tacos for dinner. Beverage service: YOYO. No hard alcohol allowed. No corkage fee.
(773) 327-5240, www.papacitosrestaurant.com, 9–10 every day

PASSAGE TO INDIA $$

4609 N. Lincoln (Wilson), **Lincoln Square**
Indian/Vegetarian-Friendly

New owners (formerly Anatolian Kabob) offer an extensive Indian menu that covers a lot of ground, from samosas and tandoori to chicken tikka masala and spicy vindaloo. There are ten freshly baked breads in addition to the traditional naan. They provide wine and beer glasses and servers will open bottles. No corkage fee.
(773) 561-2200, Mon–Sat 11:30–10, Sun closed

PENNY'S NOODLE SHOP $

3400 N. Sheffield (Roscoe), **Lakeview**
Pan-Asian

In 1989, owners opened up Penny's with designs to "Western-ize Thai food." Almost 20 years and four locations later, I'd say they've succeeded. This is the only location that's BYOB, as the city mandates at least two bathrooms for a liquor license. They provide rocks and highball glasses and corkscrews and will put your stash in the cooler. No corkage fee.
(773) 281-8222, www.pennysnoodleshop.com, Mon closed, Tues–Thurs 11–10, Fri–Sat 11–10:30, Sun 11–10 🐦

PHO 888 $$
1137 W. Argyle (Broadway), Uptown
Vietnamese
If you can't decide what to order among the nearly 170 menu items, start with the crispy pancake as an appetizer, then move on to the pho (beef noodle soup) and you can't miss. They provide water glasses. No corkage fee.
(773) 907-8838, Mon 9–2, Tues–Thurs 9–9, Fri–Sun 9–10

PHOENIX INN $
608 Davis (Chicago), Evanston
Chinese/Vegetarian-Friendly
New owners took over this downtown Evanston eatery recently and woke up this small space by painting the walls bright green and yellow. The menu still features standard Chinese fare, with plenty of vegetarian options. They provide water glasses and corkscrews. No corkage fee.
(847) 475-7782, www.phoenix608.com, Mon–Thurs 11–9:30, Fri–Sat 11–10, Sun 12–9:30

PINGPONG $$
3322 N. Broadway (Roscoe), Lakeview
Pan-Asian
This once tight space recently expanded to seat about 50; now it feels more restaurant/nightclub and less elbow-to-elbow café. The ultra-modern, white-on-white surroundings offer a hip feel that matches the menu, which features contemporary twists on sushi, Thai, Chinese, and other Asian cuisines. There are rumors that a liquor license may be on the way, so double-check it's still BYOB. They provide wine glasses, ice buckets, and servers open bottles. There's a fee of $2 per table to recycle your bottles.
(773) 281-7575, www.pingpongrestaurant.com, 4–12 every day 🐦

PINTO THAI KITCHEN $

1931 Central (Green Bay), Evanston
Thai/Chinese

New owners transformed this former Chinese restaurant into a
cute, contemporary Thai spot (but kept 20% of the Chinese menu
to "transition" regulars). Expect specials such as mango chicken,
sautéed black mussels, and rotating seasonal seafood entrées.
They provide wine glasses, chilled pilsner glasses, ice buckets,
and corkscrews. No corkage fee.

(847) 328-8881, www.pintokitchen.com, 11:30–9:30 every day

PIZZA RUSTICA $$

3913 N. Sheridan (Irving), Lakeview
Italian/Pizza

This neighborhood café is a true gem, not only for its cute décor
and reasonable prices, but also its delicious, authentic Italian
food. Highlights include the crispy, flaky, Italian pizza; daily
specials; and freshly made pastas—and you never know what
celeb might walk in. They provide wine glasses and Champagne
buckets and will open your bottles upon request.

(773) 404-8955, www.pizzarusticachicago.com, Sun–Mon 11–10,
Tues closed, Wed–Thurs 11–10, Fri–Sat 11–11 ☂

POT PAN $

1750 W. North (Wood), Bucktown
Thai/Vegetarian-Friendly

An ex-Benihana chef whips up affordable, fresh Thai food in a relaxing atmosphere with tasteful décor. They provide wine glasses,
beer mugs, Champagne flutes, and ice buckets. No corkage fee (as
long as each person orders an entrée).

(773) 862-6990, www.potpanthai.com, Mon–Thurs 11–10, Fri–Sat
11–11, Sun 12–10

PREAW WHAN $

1025 W. Lawrence (Kenmore), Uptown
Thai

The ownership has changed (used to be Thai Super Chef), but the
same chef is here, and the décor has been slightly updated at this
strip-mall eatery. They provide wine glasses and corkscrews. No
corkage fee.

(773) 784-6169, Mon closed, Tues–Thurs 11–9, Fri–Sat 11–10,
Sun 11–9 Ⓟ

QUEEN OF SHEBA CAFÉ $$
5403 N. Broadway (Balmoral), Edgewater
Ethiopian/Vegetarian-Friendly
Garish art and a boombox blaring Europop greet you as you walk
into this small eatery, but don't come here for the atmosphere—
this storefront on busy Broadway is a popular spot for authentic
Ethiopian cuisine. They provide wine glasses and corkscrews. No
corkage fee.
(773) 878-2352, 3:30–11 every day

RANALLI'S UP NORTH $$
1522 W. Montrose (Ashland), Uptown
Italian/Pizza/Mexican
Owners have made recent improvements to the dining room and
outdoor patio, giving you all the more reason to check out this
quirky space. The menu boasts 50 ingredients for your pizza (all
ingredients are free after the fourth!) as well as Italian entrées and
sandwiches. They provide rocks glasses, and servers will open
your bottles. No corkage fee.
(773) 506-8800, www.ranallisupnorth.com, Sun–Thurs 11–12,
Fri–Sat 11–2a

RHYTHM AND SPICE $$
2501 W. 79th (Campbell), South Shore
Jamaican/Caribbean
Located within 100 feet of a school, this Jamaican spot is BYOB
indefinitely. They may not be able to serve you a drink, but they
do offer seafood served six ways, jerk chicken, plantains, and
banana bread—all in a friendly atmosphere with Jamaican music
in the background. They provide wine glasses and corkscrews.
Corkage fees may apply for large groups.
(773) 476-5600, www.rhythmandspicerestaurant.com, Mon
closed, Tues–Thurs 11–8, Fri–Sat 11–10, Sun 11–8

RICK'S CAFÉ CASABLANCA $$$$

3915 N. Sheridan (Irving Park Rd.), Lakeview
French/Italian

This is a favorite destination for many BYOB diners. The classy dining room and outdoor patio provide an elegant backdrop for the upscale cuisine, which is a combination of mostly French and some Italian and Spanish influences. They provide wine glasses, decanters, Champagne flutes, and ice buckets. Servers will open bottles (and even serve cheese as you sip your vino).

(773) 327-1972, Mon closed, Tues–Sun 5–11, reservations recommended on weekends 🏴

RIQUE'S REGIONAL MEXICAN FOOD $$

5004 N. Sheridan (Argyle), Uptown
Mexican/Brunch

If a small Mexican BYOB in a mostly Asian neighborhood makes it on the "best restaurants in Chicago" list in *GQ*, there must be something special going on. Small plates, soups, and entrées highlight regional Mexican cuisine, made-to-order with fresh and simple ingredients. The private party room in back accommodates 29. Customers can bring in Bloody Mary mix, vodka, and tequila. They provide wine stemware, bistro-style glasses, Champagne flutes, corkscrews, limes, and will put beer in the fridge. No corkage fee.

(773) 728-6200, www.riqueschicago.com, Mon–Tues 4–10, Wed–Sat 11–11, Sun 10–11, reservations recommended

ROBINSON'S NO. 1 RIBS LINCOLN PARK $$

655 W. Armitage (Orchard), Lincoln Park
BBQ/American

Owners recently remodeled for a more modern, clean look. In addition to its top-rated ribs, Robinson's also offers seafood and chicken dinners, burgers, and salads. The outdoor patio is a popular spot for parties (kegs are allowed). They provide red wine glasses, chilled white wine glasses, chilled pilsner glasses, ice buckets, and corkscrews. No corkage fee (with purchase of entrée).

(312) 337-1399, www.ribs1.com, Mon closed, Tues–Thurs 4–9, Fri–Sun 4–10 🏴

ROONG PETCH $
1828 W. Montrose (Ravenswood), Lincoln Square
Thai
For over 20 years, Roong Petch has served authentic Thai dishes
such as crab Rangoon, pad Thai, and nam sod (steamed ground
pork with lemon juice, peanuts, hot peppers, and green onions)
to the Ravenswood neighborhood. They provide water glasses, an
ice bucket (yes, there's only one), and corkscrews. No corkage fee.
(773) 989-0818, www.roongpetch.com, Mon–Thurs 11:30–9:30,
Fri–Sat 11:30–10, Sun closed

ROSATI'S $
126 W. Grand (LaSalle), River North
Pizza/Italian
This Rosati's location serves pizza for all tastes—thin, double-
dough, stuffed, or deep dish—plus the obligatory Italian
sandwiches, pastas, and salads. Their dining room accommodates
about 25 inside and 25 more on the outdoor patio, weather
permitting. They provide plastic cups and corkscrews and even
keep your bottles in a cooler. No corkage fee.
(312) 755-9955, www.rosatispizza.com, Sun–Thurs 10:30–9:30,
Fri–Sat 12–11 🪁

ROSDED $
2308 W. Leland (Lincoln), Lincoln Square
Thai
There is no shortage of Thai restaurants in this neighborhood,
but Rosded has remained a neighborhood favorite since 1976,
owing to its extensive menu of traditional and unique Thai
dishes—many of them seafood-based. There's a metered parking
lot across the street. They provide water glasses. No corkage fee.
(773) 334-9055, Mon closed, Tues–Sat 11:30–9, Sun 12–8:30

ROYAL THAI $
2209 W. Montrose (Lincoln), Lincoln Square
Thai/Vegetarian-Friendly
The updated décor, mesmerizing fish tank, and soothing background music set a serene scene. They feature daily specials and
the usual Thai suspects. The owners do not believe in consuming
or serving alcohol, but they do allow customers to BYOB. Beverage service: YOYO. No corkage fee.
(773) 509-0007, Mon–Thurs 11:30–9:30, Fri–Sat 11:30–10, Sun 12–9

RUBY OF SIAM $$

9420 Skokie Blvd. (Golf), Skokie

Thai

BYOB is trés popular here, evident in the above-average beverage service. Plus, the silk tapestries, intricate wood carvings, and gentle Thai music playing in the background serve as pleasant distractions from the busy strip-mall location. They provide wine glasses, chilled beer mugs, and Champagne buckets, and servers will open your bottles. No corkage fee.

(847) 675-7008, www.rubyofsiam.com, Mon–Thurs 11–10, Fri–Sat 11–11, Sun 12–10

RUDY'S TASTE $$

1024 N. Ashland (Augusta), East Ukrainian Village

Caribbean/Guatemalan/Mexican

Rudy's serves three complete menus of Caribbean, Guatemalan, and Mexican cuisine. As if that didn't make the choices hard enough, there are low-priced (*paches de papas*, tacos) and more upscale (chicken in mole sauce, strip steak) offerings. They provide wine glasses and corkscrews. No corkage fee.

(773) 252-3666, Mon–Tues 11–10, Wed 5–10, Thurs–Sat 11–10, Sun 11–9

SABOR A CUBA $$

1833 W. Wilson (Wolcott), Lincoln Square

Cuban

Authentic, homemade Cuban cuisine is the specialty here, served in a homey, lively atmosphere geared toward large parties. Mojito and margarita mixes are in the works, perfect for your stash of rum or tequila. They provide wine glasses, ice buckets, and corkscrews. No corkage fee.

(773) 769-6859, Mon closed, Tues–Thurs 10–10, Fri–Sat 10–11, Sun 10–9, reservations recommended

SAI MAI THAI RESTAURANT $

2532 N. California (Logan Blvd.), Logan Square
Thai

The owners opened up this casual neighborhood spot in 2004
with no plans to obtain a liquor license anytime soon. Bonus: you
can run right next door for an affordable bottle of boutique wine.
They provide juice and water glasses and will put your bottles in
the cooler. No corkage fee.

(773) 276-8424, Mon–Thurs 11–9:30, Fri 11–10:30, Sat 12–
10:30, Sun 12–9

SAN CHAE DOL SOT RESTAURANT $$

3737B W. Lawrence (Ridgeway), Albany Park
Korean

This small, friendly place serves an extensive menu of authentic
Korean fare. Beginners should go for the *san chae jung sik* special—
rice individually cooked in a stone pot with a large variety of
Korean fish and veggies. There's a $20 credit card minimum. They
provide beer mugs, water glasses, Korean wine glasses, and rocks
glasses. No corkage fee.

(773) 588-5223, Thurs–Tues 10:30–10:30, Wed closed Ⓟ

SATAY $$

936 W. Diversey (Sheffield), Lakeview
Pan-Asian/Sushi

Step inside and you'll feel like you've walked into an IKEA
showroom. Then it's decision time: there are 138 dishes to choose
from, many of them unexpected, such as Indian-style pancakes
(roti and yellow curry) and roasted duck with blackberry sauce.
They provide wine glasses. No corkage fee.

(773) 477-0100, Sun–Mon 4–10, Tues–Thurs 11–10, Fri–Sat
11–11

SCHWA $$$$
1466 N. Ashland (LeMoyne), Wicker Park
Eclectic
Chef Michael Carlson reclaimed this tiny, 26-seat dining room (formerly occupied by Lovitt) as Schwa, which is defined in *Webster's* as an "unstressed vowel." Carlson, who was featured in *Food & Wine* magazine's "Best New Chef 2006" issue, offers two tasting menus: $55 for three courses, $90 for nine. The esoteric dishes include quail egg ravioli and sablefish with pineapple, macadamia nuts, taro root, and prosciutto. They provide bistro-style glasses.
(773) 252-1466, www.schwarestaurant.com, Sun–Mon closed, Tues–Sat 5:30–10:30, reservations required

SEMIRAMIS $$
4639–41 N. Kedzie (Wilson), Albany Park
Middle Eastern
Owner Joseph Abraham (formerly of Leo's Lunchroom) makes a mean shawerma (rotisserie chicken, lamb, or beef with eggplant, red cabbage, tomatoes, hummus, cucumber, and tahini sauce on a pita). Located steps from the Kedzie stop on the Brown Line. They provide wine glasses and ice buckets, and servers will open your wine.
(773) 279-8900, Mon–Sat 11–10, Sun closed

SHER-A-PUNJAB $$
2510 W. Devon (Maplewood), West Rogers Park
Indian
Sher-A-Punjab features Thali, a traditional style of Indian dining in which diners sample a full vegetarian, meat, or seafood menu—from appetizers to dessert—for around only $13 each. The tantalizing buffet is also available for $8.95. They provide wine glasses. No corkage fee.
(773) 973-4000, 11–11 every day, reservations recommended on weekends

SHUI WAH $$
2162A S. Archer (Cermak), Chinatown
Chinese

By day this small place in Chinatown Square serves made-to-
order dim sum. But at night a different chef takes over the kitchen
and serves chui-chow style cooking. If shark-fin soup or chicken
feet aren't your thang, there are plenty of Anglo-friendly dishes
like fried rice and sweet-and-sour chicken to keep you happy.
They provide water glasses. No corkage fee.
(312) 225-8811, 8–3 (dim sum), 5–2 (dinner) every day

SIAM COUNTRY $
4637 N. Damen (Wilson), Lincoln Square
Thai

Everything is made-to-order here, including the popular Thai
BBQ pork spare ribs with garlic sauce. There's a liquor store next
door for convenience. They provide corkscrews and will put your
bottles in the fridge upon request. No corkage fee.
(773) 271-0700, www.siamcountrychicago.com, Thurs–Tues
11:30–10, Wed closed 🏃

SIAM NOODLE & RICE $
4654 N. Sheridan (Wilson), Uptown
Thai

Customers love the homemade sauces (ginger, peanut, and others)
so much that they order sticky rice and start dippin'. They provide
wine glasses, ice buckets, and corkscrews. No corkage fee.
(773) 769-6694, www.siamnoodleandrice.com, Mon closed,
Tues–Thurs 11–9, Fri 11–9:30, Sat 11:30–9:30, Sun 11:30–8
(closed every day from 4–5)

SIAM RICE THAI CUISINE $$
117 N. Wells (Washington), Loop
Thai

This large dining room, filled with dark wood and simple décor,
is a great option for a weekday dinner in the Loop that won't
break your budget. Garage parking next door is about ten bucks.
They provide wine glasses, ice buckets, and corkscrews. No
corkage fee.
(312) 606-9999, www.siamricethai.com, Mon–Fri 11–8,
Sat–Sun closed

SIAM TASTE NOODLE $

4323 W. Addison (Milwaukee), Old Irving Park
Thai/Vegetarian-Friendly

The owner/chef at this casual, cute eatery has been cooking Thai
for over 30 years in both Thailand and the U.S. She uses only
vegetable oil, no MSG, and will prepare any dish vegetarian. The
menu features more seafood dishes than most Thai places. They
provide wine glasses and corkscrews. No corkage fee.
(773) 286-6020, http://siamtaste.net, Mon–Sat 11–10, Sun 4–9

SINBAD'S FINE MEDITERRANEAN GRILL $$

444 W. Fullerton (Clark), Lincoln Park
Mediterranean

Located below sidewalk level, this new, inviting BYOB offers
Mediterranean standards (tabouleh, falafel, kabobs), Moroccan
tagine (slow-cooked stew of meat and veggies), and combination
plates for sampling. Mediterranean artifacts accent the walls and
ceiling. They provide wine glasses and corkscrews. No corkage fee.
(773) 525-2233, www.sinbadsgrill.com, Mon–Thurs 11–10,
Fri–Sat 11–11, Sun 12–8 🥢

SNAIL THAI CUISINE $

1649 E. 55th (Hyde Park Blvd.), Hyde Park
Thai

Not your typical Thai takeout joint. Since the early '90s, the
neighborhood has been taken with Snail's made-from-scratch
saikrok e-sarn (Northeastern Thai-style sausages with ginger, green
chili, and roasted peanuts), pork dumplings, and other traditional
fare. They provide wine glasses, chilled beer mugs, ice buckets,
and corkscrews. No corkage fee.
(773) 667-5423, www.snailthai.com, Tues–Sun 11–10, Mon closed

SO GONG DONG TOFU RESTAURANT $

3307 W. Bryn Mawr (Kedzie), North Park
Korean

The dark-wood dining room has a few private alcoves for small
parties, but get there early before they're taken. Dishes include
Korean pancakes (with scallions, seafood, and peppers) and
healthy fare such as steamed dumplings, many tofu-based soups,
and bibimbop, served in a hot stone pot. They have water glasses
on hand. No corkage fee.
(773) 539-8377, Thurs–Tues 10–10, Wed closed

SOL DE MEXICO $$

3018 N. Cicero (Wellington), Cragin
Mexican

This promising new BYOB offers Mexican small plates for
around $8 each and a host of seafood or meat entrées. The most
talked-about items on the menu are the made-from-scratch mole
sauces—each one reflecting a different Mexican region's cuisine.
They provide wine glasses, pilsner glasses, martini glasses, and ice
buckets. No corkage fee.

(773) 282-4119, Mon, Wed–Sat 11–10, Sun 11–9, Tues closed

SPEAKEASY SUPPER CLUB $$$$

1401 W. Devon (Glenwood), Edgewater
Eclectic

There aren't many BYOBs that have white and red wine glasses
at each place setting, a live music cabaret, or an actual bar where
you can sip your own drinks. Speakeasy has all three. Owned by
Michael Feinstein and Jody Andre, former owner of Tomboy and
South, Speakeasy has three rooms to enjoy live music, fine dining,
or both. The first room is a "bar," where you can relax, unwind,
and order food in a casual atmosphere. The simple, elegant dining
room is set with white linen tablecloths and candlelight. Finally,
the cabaret—complete with a stage and grand piano—also has
dinner seating and live music and is popular for large parties.
Highlights on the menu include duck cassoulet, lamp chops, filet
mignon, and pecan-crusted grouper. They provide white and red
wine glasses, martini glasses, shakers, and ice buckets and will
open your bottles.

(773) 338-0600, www.speakeasysupperclub.com, Mon
closed, Tues–Thurs 5–9, Fri–Sat 5–11, Sun 5–10, reservations
recommended (especially on nights with live music) Ⓟ ♪

THE SPICE THAI CUISINE $

2886 N. Milwaukee (Diversey), Logan Square
Thai/Vegetarian-Friendly

You'll either find the odd décor here quirky or charming (or
both). In any case, stir-fry is Spice Thai's specialty, and dishes are
prepared as spicy as you can tolerate. They provide wine glasses
and ice buckets. No corkage fee.

(773) 252-9959, Sun–Mon 4–10, Tues–Sat 11:30–10

SPOON THAI $

4608 N. Western (Wilson), Lincoln Square
Thai

Not a lot of people BYOB here, but it is welcome, and the food is consistently high rated. They provide wine glasses, and servers will put your bottles in the fridge upon request. No corkage fee.
(773) 769-1173, www.spoonthai.com, 11–10 every day

SPRING WORLD $$

2109A S. China Place (Cermak), Chinatown
Chinese

Expect attentive service at this small place, nestled in the Chinatown Square, an open-air mall of restaurants, pharmacies, groceries, and other businesses. The menu draws from Shanghai, Peking, Szechuan, and Yunan cuisine, but regulars rave about the "Across the Bridge," or Yunan rice noodle. They provide water glasses. No corkage fee.
(312) 326-9966, Mon–Thurs 11–10, Fri–Sun 10–10

STANDARD INDIA $$

917 W. Belmont (Clark), Lakeview
Indian/Vegetarian-Friendly

Here, it's all about the buffet, where you can fill up on tasty samosas, tandoori, naan, and more. The mango shake is a cold, creamy drink for nondrinking dinner companions and offers a cool antidote to the curry. They provide water glasses and corkscrews.
(773) 929-1123, www.standardindia.com, 12–3 every day (lunch), Sun–Thurs 5–10, Fri–Sat 5–11 (dinner)

STATE RESTAURANT & CAFÉ $$$

935 W. Webster (Sheffield), Lincoln Park
Contemporary American

Their liquor license is pending indefinitely, so BYOB while you can. This classy joint offers upscale, contemporary American favorites. Every item on the menu is half off on Mondays and Wednesdays. Half-priced food and BYOB? Maybe you can save for college. They provide a full array of glassware and chilling devices and will open your bottles. No corkage fee.
(773) 975-8030, www.statechicago.com, Mon–Thurs 10:30–10, Fri 10:30–11, Sat 9:30–11, Sun 9:30–10

STICKY RICE $
4018 N. Western (Irving Park Rd.), North Center
Thai
This Northern Thai place is famous for its *sai ma*, or Thai sausage.
There are daily specials and a separate Thai menu with an English
translation. They provide wine glasses, Champagne flutes, beer
glasses, ice buckets, and corkscrews and will put your bottles in
the cooler upon request. No corkage fee.
(773) 588-0133, www.stickyricethai.com, Mon–Thurs 11:30–11,
Fri–Sat 11:30–12, Sun 12–10

SULTAN'S MARKET $
2057 W. North (Hoyne), Wicker Park
Middle Eastern/Mediterranean/Vegetarian-Friendly
You will rarely find anyone who BYOBs here, but it is allowed.
And if you have not stood in line for one of their now-famous
falafel sandwiches, slathered in homemade hummus, you have not
done falafel. Beverage service: YOYO. No corkage fee (obviously).
(773) 235-3072, www.chicagofalafel.com, Mon–Sat 10–9, Sun
10–7, wi-fi access 📶 🏧

SUNSHINE CAFÉ $$
5449 N. Clark (Balmoral), Andersonville
Japanese
Generous bowls of broth brimming with noodles, vegetables,
and meat are the specialty at this traditional Japanese eatery, a
neighborhood mainstay long before the surrounding chic shops
and cafés opened. They provide sake cups and corkscrews and
will put your bottles in the fridge. No corkage fee.
(773) 334-6214, Mon closed, Tues–Sun 12–9

SUSHI 28 CAFÉ $$$
2863 N. Clark (Diversey), Lakeview
Sushi/Japanese
Owners honed their culinary skills at the Peninsula Hotel in
Chicago before opening up this casual sushi bar. Leave your mark
by adding to the collection of empty bottles on the window sill.
They provide wine glasses, Champagne flutes, and corkscrews and
will open your bottles or put them in the cooler upon request. No
corkage fee.
(773) 868-1250, www.sushi28cafe.com, Sun–Thurs 12:30–10,
Fri–Sat 12–10:30, Tues closed 🏧

SUSHI II PARA $$$
2256 N. Clark (Webster), Lincoln Park
Japanese/Sushi

You'll find sushi, maki, sashimi, Japanese entrées, and all-you-can-eat specials in a traditional Japanese setting at this casual, 30-seat subterranean spot. Upon request they will provide wine glasses, sake cups, and sake pitchers and warm up your sake in the microwave. No corkage fee.

(773) 477-3219, Mon–Thurs 11–10, Fri–Sat 11–10:30, Sun 12:30–9:30

SUSHI X $$$
1136 W. Chicago (Racine), River West
Sushi

Blink and you'll miss the jet-black building that houses this casual but cool sushi spot. Sushi X mostly does takeout business, which may explain why it's BYOB, but inside is a dark, modern dining room that seats about 25. The menu includes hot and cold appetizers, including oyster shooters. They provide juice glasses and ice buckets. No corkage fee.

(312) 491-9232, www.sushi-x.net, Mon–Fri 11–2, 5–12, Sat 5–12, Sun 5–11

SWEET TAMARIND $$
1408 W. Diversey (Southport), Lakeview
Thai

Named after a fruit juice used in Thai cooking, Sweet Tamarind serves Thai food that's several notches above ordinary, especially the tamarind curry and walnut-and-raisin fried rice. A liquor license has been pending for many months (years?), but BYOB will be allowed either way. They provide wine glasses, pilsner glasses, and corkscrews. No corkage fee.

(773) 281-5300, www.sweettamarindcuisine.com, Sun–Thurs 11:30–10, Fri–Sat 11:30–11 ✈

TABOUN GRILL $$$
6339 N. California (Devon), West Rogers Park
Middle Eastern/Israeli/Brunch
Named for the traditional clay oven used for baking pita,
Taboun offers delicious, nutritious kosher cuisine. Only kosher
wine is allowed; look for "mevushal" on the bottle; any type of
beer or spirits is okay. Sunday features Yeminite brunch from
11–3. They provide water glasses and will open your bottles.
No corkage fee.
(773) 381-2606, www.taboungrill.com, Sun–Thurs 11–10, Fri
11–3, Sat closed (seasonal) Ⓟ

TAGINE $$
4749 N. Rockwell (Lawrence), Ravenswood
Moroccan
Celebrated chef Eddie Maettaoui (NoMi, Avenue) offers traditional Moroccan cuisine at this new BYOB. In addition to the
namesake dish, Maettaoui serves couscous entrées, lamb and
chicken dishes, and vegetarian options. They provide red and
white wine stemware, beer mugs, Champagne flutes, ice buckets,
and corkscrews. No corkage fee.
(773) 989-4340, www.chicagotagine.com, Mon–Thurs 4–10, Fri
4–11, Sat 12–11, Sun 12–9 🐾

TANGO SUR $$$
3763 N. Southport (Grace), Lakeview
Argentinian
This is one of the more upscale BYOBs in Chicago and serves as
a great place for either large parties or intimate dates. The details
here are authentically Argentinian, from the simple décor to the
parrillada (meat served on a tabletop grill). They provide wine
glasses, pilsner glasses, and wine chillers and will open your
bottles. No corkage fee.
(773) 477-5466, 5–10:30 every day, reservations recommended 🐾

TANK RESTAURANT $$
4953–55 N. Broadway (Argyle), Uptown
Vietnamese

All members of Uptown's diverse community intersect here,
lapping up steaming bowls of pho and sharing Vietnamese
favorites family-style at all hours of the day. The atmosphere is
more in keeping with a busy, 24-hour coffee shop. They provide
corkscrews. No corkage fee.

(773) 878-2253, Mon–Sat 8:30–10, Sun 8:30–9, Wed closed

TANOSHII $$$
5547 N. Clark (Bryn Mawr), Edgewater
Sushi

Celebrated sushi chef and owner "Sushi Mike" prepares customized sushi, based not only on your individual tastes but also the
catches of the day. Park free at the Salvation Army lot on the
weekends. They provide wine glasses, sake cups, and ice buckets
and will warm up your sake in hot water, open your bottles, and
put them in the cooler upon request.

(773) 878-6886, www.tanoshiichicago.com, Sun–Mon 4–10,
Tues closed, Wed–Thurs 4–11, Fri 4–12, Sat 2–12, reservations
recommended

TASTE OF PERU $$
6545 N. Clark (Arthur), Rogers Park
Peruvian

The no-frills strip-mall location belies an authentic, family-run
eatery that boasts generous portions and live music on the
weekends. The "blue plates" include fried red snapper with garlic
cream sauce over rice and lobster tail in white wine, beer, and
Peruvian brandy (gee, maybe BYOB isn't necessary). They provide
wine glasses, ice buckets, and corkscrews.

(773) 381-4540, www.tasteofperu.com, Sun–Thurs 11:30–10,
Fri–Sat 11:30–11 🅿 ♫

TERRAGUSTO $$$
1851 W. Addison (Wolcott), Lakeview
Italian

Theo Gilbert (Trattoria No. 10, Spiaggia) offers café-style dining
in a mostly residential area of West Lakeview. Pasta is made every
day in the front window, and at night Gilbert prepares simple,
tasty pasta dishes, meats, salads, and desserts. They provide
bistro-style glasses, Champagne flutes, and wine chillers, and
servers will open your bottles. No corkage fee.

(773) 248-2777, Tues–Sun 5:30–9:30, Mon closed, reservations
recommended 🎏

THAI 55 $
1607 E. 55th (Cornell), Hyde Park
Thai

Wood-paneled walls lend to the relaxing atmosphere here, touted
as the "oldest Thai restaurant in Hyde Park." The food is prepared
for "non-Thai" customers (i.e., not too much heat). They provide
wine glasses, chilled beer mugs, and corkscrews. No corkage fee.

(773) 363-7119, www.thai55restaurant.com, 11–10 every day

THAI AREE $$
3592 N. Milwaukee (Addison), Old Irving Park
Thai

This family-owned spot has served the northwest side for over 20
years, though now just for dinner. The small dining room is cozy
and relaxing, and the menu is extensive. You'll find customers
here who have moved away but came back for the shrimp in
blanket, Thai sausages, and som tum salad. They provide water
glasses, ice buckets (for bottles and glasses—who knew?), and
corkscrews. No corkage fee.

(773) 725-6751, Mon–Sat 4–9, Sun closed

THAI AROMA $

4142 N. Broadway (Buena), Uptown
Thai

All three Thai Aroma locations feature traditional Thai favorites and daily specials such as spicy catfish and pad Thai duck. Only the Uptown and Old Town locations are BYOB. This one, on Broadway, features parking and a cute, contemporary atmosphere. They provide wine glasses, pint glasses, ice buckets, and servers will open your bottles. No corkage fee.

(773) 404-9386, www.aromachicago.com, Sun–Thurs 11–10, Fr–Sat 11–11 Ⓟ

THAI AROMA $

417 W. North (Sedgwick), Old Town
Thai

This new location just opened in summer 2006. You have to chuckle at their "outdoor seating": two chairs and a small table placed on the sidewalk on either side of a parking meter. Are diners ticketed if they don't feed the meter? They provide wine glasses, pint glasses, and ice buckets, and servers will open your bottles. No corkage fee.

(312) 664-3400, www.aromachicago.com, Sun–Thurs 11–10, Fr–Sat 11–11

THAI AVENUE $

4949 N. Broadway (Argyle), Uptown
Thai

Among a plethora of Asian restaurants in this area, Thai Avenue offers something a little different: made-to-order Thai food that reflects the dishes you can buy on the street in Thailand. They provide wine glasses and corkscrews (and interesting parfait glasses for beer). No corkage fee.

(773) 878-2222, Mon–Thurs 11–9:30, Fri–Sat 11–10, Sun 11–9

THAI BINH $$

1113 W. Argyle (Winthrop), Uptown
Vietnamese

Traditional Vietnamese noodle soups, rice dishes, and more are all served family-style here. They provide wine glasses and ice buckets and will put your bottles in the cooler. No corkage fee.

(773) 728-0283, 11–11 every day

THAI CLASSIC $
3332 N. Clark (Roscoe), Lakeview
Thai

Since 1989, this Lakeview institution, with its traditional Thai seating, has proved popular for birthdays and other celebrations. Rumor has it they may be applying for a liquor license, but they've been saying that for years. Don't forget to take off your shoes at the door. They provide wine glasses. No corkage fee.
(773) 404-2000, www.thaiclassicrestaurant.com, 11:30–10 every day

THAI EATERY $
2234 N. Western (Lyndale), Logan Square
Thai

This tiny eatery in West Bucktown offers a comprehensive menu of Thai appetizers, salads, soups, rice and noodle dishes, and entrées. The 30-seat dining room is cute and the staff is friendly. They provide wine glasses, pint glasses, and corkscrews. No corkage fee.
(773) 394-3035, Mon closed, Tues–Sat 11:30–10, Sun 4–10

THAI GRILL $
1040 W. Granville (Kenmore), Edgewater
Thai/Pan-Asian/Vegetarian-Friendly

Parking's tough around here, but there's a free lot across the street. Popular Thai dishes and a "special" Thai menu (furnished upon request) are both available. The party room accommodates 20–50 guests and is private, should you feel the need to break out the karaoke machine. They provide wine glasses and will open your bottles. No corkage fee.
(773) 274-7510, Mon closed, Tues–Sun 11:30–10 🅿

THAI KITCHEN $
1513 W. Irving Park Rd. (Ashland), Lakeview
Thai

Located across the street from a school, this new neighborhood spot is BYOB indefinitely. The nightly specials are the highlight here, from steamed mussels to roast duck. There's parking behind the restaurant (huge plus in this area). Dessert glasses are your only options for wine and beer, but they will keep your bottles in the cooler. No corkage fee.
(773) 472-9090, www.yourthaikitchen.com, Mon–Thurs 11–10, Fri–Sat 11–11, Sun 4–10 🅿

THAI LAGOON $

2322 W. North (Western), Bucktown
Thai/Sushi

This west Bucktown eatery combines traditional Thai food with
contemporary ambience (techno plays in the background at a
conversation-friendly level). The menu includes such entrées as
sesame-crusted tuna steak in orange, ginger, and lemongrass and
a limited sushi selection on the weekends. They provide water
glasses and ice buckets and will open bottles.

(773) 489-5747, Sun–Thurs 5–10, Fri–Sat 5–11

THAI LINDA CAFÉ $$

2022 W. Roscoe (Damen), Roscoe Village
Thai

The décor was recently updated with both Thai and modern
touches, giving this neighborhood place a much-needed face-lift.
The spicy duck and pad Thai are highlights here. They provide
wine glasses, ice buckets, and corkscrews. No corkage fee.

(773) 868-0075, www.thailinda.com, Mon–Thurs 11–9:30, Fri–Sat
11–10, Sun 4–9:30 ⏶

THAI ME UP $

434 W. Diversey (Sheridan), Lakeview
Thai

Choose from spicy, nonspicy, low-fat, and vegetarian versions
of Thai noodle and rice dishes, from the same owners of Satay
(another BYOB just down the street). They have an odd assortment of wine and margarita glasses on hand. No corkage fee.

(773) 404-1178, Mon delivery only, Tues–Thurs 11–10, Fri–Sat
11–11, Sun 4–10

THAI ON CLARK $

4641 N. Clark (Wilson), Ravenswood
Thai

This is a family-friendly, casual neighborhood eatery that serves
up traditional Thai cuisine at reasonable prices. They provide
juice glasses, ice buckets, and corkscrews. No corkage fee.

(773) 275-2620, Sun–Thurs 11–9:30, Fri–Sat 11–10

THAI OSCAR $$
4638 N. Western (Wilson), Lincoln Square
Japanese/Sushi/Thai

It would take days to get through Thai Oscar's extensive Thai and
Japanese menu, which reflects the owner's mixed ancestry. Choose
from safe bets such as pad Thai and teriyaki or specialty dishes
and sushi for more adventuresome tastes. They provide wine
glasses, beer mugs, sake cups, sake pitchers, and ice buckets and
will warm up your sake in the microwave or put your bottles in
the fridge upon request. No corkage fee.

(773) 878-5922, www.thaioscar.com, Mon–Thurs 11–10, Fri–Sat
11–11, Sun 4-10

THAI PASTRY $$
4925 N. Broadway (Ainslie), Uptown
Thai

Aumphai Kusab's vibrant pastry-shop-turned-restaurant gets
packed on the weekends but is definitely worth the wait. The
showcased treats are homemade on-site. They provide wine
glasses. No corkage fee.

(773) 784-5399, www.thaipastry.com, Sun–Thurs 11–10, Fri–Sat
11–11, reservations recommended 🔺

THAI SPICE $$
1320 W. Devon (Wayne), Rogers Park
Thai/Sushi

Owner Anthony Hubich declares his Thai mother-in-law the
"secret weapon" at this cute eatery. She takes no shortcuts with
the food, using only authentic Thai recipes and fresh ingredients.
Portions are big enough to share. The charming dining rooms
feature some traditional Thai floor seating (with comfy cushions).
Worth the trip up to the far north side. They provide wine glasses,
ice buckets, and corkscrews. No corkage fee.

(773) 973-0504, Mon closed, Tues–Thurs 4–10, Fri–Sat 4–11, Sun
4–10

THAI VALLEY $
4600 N. Kedzie (Wilson), Albany Park
Thai

Even in the middle of a weekday afternoon, this place can pack
'em in. They feature traditional Thai favorites (pad Thai, crab
Rangoon, larb) along with a few you don't see very often, such as
gang ped phed, a dish made with roast duck, coconut milk, red
curry, and pineapple. Beverage service: YOYO. No corkage fee.
(773) 588-2020, Mon closed, Tues–Sun 11:30–10

THAI VILLAGE $
2053 W. Division (Damen), Wicker Park
Thai

Thai Village was serving the Wicker Park neighborhood long
before real estate prices skyrocketed. The large, sun-drenched
outdoor patio is a great place to enjoy generous helpings of pad
Thai or pad se ewe, sip a glass of wine, and watch the crowds
walk by on a warm summer evening. They provide wine glasses
and rocks glasses. No corkage fee.
(773) 384-5352, Mon closed, Tues–Sun 11:30–9:30 🐦

THINK $$$
2235 N. Western (Lyndale), Bucktown
Contemporary American/Fusion/Italian

If you're looking for an upscale BYOB dining experience, look no
further than this elegant, west Bucktown spot. Owner/chef Omar
Rodriguez (ex-Carlucci group) has so many diners flocking here
for his tricolor rotini and sautéed sea scallops that he's expanded
yet again—the upstairs has been remodeled to seat an additional
45 guests. Throughout all three dining rooms, candlelight and
white linen tablecloths set the stage for a celebratory or romantic
evening, or simply a night out with friends. One bite into the
spinach and ricotta ravioli with roasted red pepper cream sauce,
the generous portion of Prince Edward Island mussels, or mouth-
watering desserts, and you'll find any excuse to come back. They
provide red and white wine glasses, Champagne flutes, rocks
glasses, martini glasses, martini shakers (BYO garnish), wine
chillers, and Champagne buckets. Servers will open your bottles.
(773) 394-0537, www.think-cafe.com, Sun–Thurs 5–10, Fri–Sat
5–11, reservations recommended every night, proper attire
required 🐦

TIEN GIANG $$
1104–06 W. Argyle (Winthrop), Uptown
Vietnamese/Chinese
If you find over 225 menu items intimidating, don't panic; the
owners, Tri and Xuan, are super friendly and will help steer you
in the right direction. They provide red and white wine glasses
(including stemless bowls), Champagne glasses, and corkscrews
and will put your stash in the cooler upon request.
(773) 275-8691, Mon–Wed 10–11, Thurs closed, Fri–Sun 9:30–11:30

TOM YUM THAI CUISINE $
3232 W. Foster (Kedzie), Albany Park
Thai/Sushi
This casual, contemporary-looking eatery sits in one of Chicago's
"dry" districts, or areas that prohibit any liquor licenses. New
owners recently added a sushi bar and bright citrus colors to the
walls for a cheery, appetizing effect. They provide wine glasses,
pilsner glasses, and corkscrews. No corkage fee.
(773) 442-8100, Mon–Thurs 11–9:30, Fri–Sat 11–10, Sun 3–9:30

TORO SUSHI $$$
2546 N. Clark (Wrightwood), Lincoln Park
Sushi
Since opening in August 2005, this neighborhood spot has
received rave reviews for its fresh, creative sushi and maki. The
space is tight, though—the dining room only seats about 20, the
sushi bar 10. They provide wine glasses and corkscrews and will
put your bottles in the fridge upon request. No corkage fee.
(773) 348-4877, Mon closed, Tues–Thurs 5–9:30, Fri–Sat
12–2:30, 5–10, Sun 4–9

TRATTORIA CATERINA $$
616 S. Dearborn (Harrison), South Loop
Italian
This is a quintessential neighborhood Italian place, where the
owners preside over the small (13-table), bustling dining room
with attentive care. The kitchen serves Old World recipes such as
stuffed clams, polenta del giorno, and chicken and veal entrées.
On weekends there's usually a wait. They provide wine glasses
and ice buckets, and servers will open your bottles.
(312) 939-7606, Mon–Thurs 11–9, Fri 11–10, Sat 5–9, Sun
closed, reservations recommended on weekends 🐀

TRE KRONOR $$$
3258 W. Foster (Kedzie), Albany Park
Scandinavian/Brunch

Tre Kronor specializes in what seems to be a dying breed in Chicago: authentic Scandinavian cuisine. Expect Swedish meatballs, Norwegian salmon, pickled herring, gravlax, the works. Many take Champagne for Sunday brunch (they offer orange juice). The private party room upstairs seats up to 35. They provide rocks glasses, frosted aquavit glasses, and ice buckets and will open bottles. No corkage fee.

(773) 267-9888, www.swedishbistro.com, Mon–Sat 7a–10p, Sun 9–3, reservations recommended every night (but not taken for weekend brunch) 🏕

TREAT $$
1616 N. Kedzie (North), Humboldt Park
Eclectic/Brunch

This bright-yellow, ultra-casual restaurant is a bright spot in an otherwise lackluster area. Moroccan and Indian influences are evident on the menu, which includes dahl makhani, chicken tikki masala, and Moroccan chicken skewers. The roasted wild mushroom appetizer is delicious, as are the desserts. They provide corkscrews and ice buckets.

(773) 772-1201, www.treatrestaurant.com, Mon, Wed–Thurs 11–9, Fri 11–10, Sat 9–10, Sun 9–9, Tues closed

TRIPI'S JOINT $$$
1467 W. Irving Park Rd. (Greenview), Lakeview
BBQ

One can only hope that Tripi's hickory-smoked barbecue transcends the "atmosphere," which, on a recent visit, was a stereo speaker on an overturned bucket and peeling purple paint. They will run to the bar next door for glasses upon request. We're talkin' bare bones here. No corkage fee.

(773) 327-0600, Mon–Thurs 12–12, Fri–Sat 12–3a, Sun 5–9

T-SPOT SUSHI AND TEA BAR $$$
3925 N. Lincoln (Irving Park Rd.), North Center
Sushi

Because the owners are focusing on their tea bar, plans for a liquor license are on the back burner. In the meantime, enjoy creative sushi and maki with a bottle of Pinot Gris in contemporary digs. They provide wine glasses, sake cups, shot glasses, ice buckets, and corkscrews and will open your bottles upon request. No corkage fee.
(773) 549-4500, www.tspotsushiandteabar.com, Mon–Thurs 12–10, Fri–Sat 12–11, Sun closed, reservations recommended on weekends

TUB TIM THAI $$
4927 Oakton (Skokie Blvd.), Skokie
Thai

With so many Thai restaurants sprouting up, it's refreshing to see unique menu items. In this case, it's the Thai crispy crepe (filled with shrimp, coconut, veggies, and peanuts) and meang kum (coconut, shrimp, ginger, lime, peanuts, and sauce wrapped in chapoo leaves), both served as appetizers. They have wine glasses on hand. No corkage fee.
(847) 675-8424, www.tubtimthai.com, Mon–Sat 11–3, 5–9, Sun closed

TURKISH CUISINE & BAKERY $$
5605 N. Clark (Bryn Mawr), Edgewater
Turkish

Six experienced chefs serve up some of the best traditional Turkish cuisine in Chicago. The place gets hopping on the weekends, with live music or belly dancing on Fridays and Saturdays. They provide wine glasses, shooters, ice buckets, and corkscrews and will open bottles or put your vodka in the freezer upon request. No corkage fee.
(773) 878-8930, www.turkishcuisine.net, 11–12 every day, reservations recommended on weekends ♫

UDUPI PALACE $$

2543 W. Devon (Rockwell), West Rogers Park
Indian/Vegetarian-Friendly

Udupi serves vegetarian-only, Southern Indian cuisine. Standouts include rasa vada (lentil donuts) and a full selection of traditional dosai, or crepes. They provide water glasses and corkscrews. No corkage fee.

(773) 338-2152, www.udupipalace.com, 11:30–10 every day

VIEN DONG $

3227 N. Clark (Belmont), Lakeview
Vietnamese/Chinese

There are over 100 dishes to choose from here, so crack open a chilled bottle of Riesling and enjoy browsing. They provide wine glasses, beer mugs, and ice buckets (but they only have two) upon request. No corkage fee.

(773) 348-6879, Mon–Thurs 11:30–10, Fri–Sat 11:30–11, Sun closed

VILLA ROSA PIZZA & PASTA $$

5345 W. Devon (Central), Edgebrook
Italian/Pizza

As owner Carlos Biedleman says, "nothing here comes from a can!" Not just a pizza takeout joint, Villa Rosa offers full pasta, risotto, ribs, and other dinners. Everything is made-to-order with fresh ingredients, from the eggplant parmigiana to the veal (prepared lemon, marsala, or vesuvio style). They provide plastic cups and corkscrews. No corkage fee.

(773) 774-7107, Sun–Thurs 10:30–10, Fri–Sat 10:30–11

WAKAMONO $$$

3317 N. Broadway (Roscoe), Lakeview
Sushi

Formerly Valhalla—a small, esoteric wine shop—this space is now a chic sushi spot, from the same owner of pingpong, across the street. Wakamono features modern and traditional takes on maki, sushi, and "japas" (Japanese small plates). They provide wine glasses, pint glasses, ice buckets, and sake cups, and servers will open bottles and heat up your sake in the microwave. No corkage fee.

(773) 296-6800, www.wakamonosushi.com, 4–12 every day 🐟

WHOLLY FRIJOLES $$
3908 W. Touhy (Crawford), Lincolnwood
Mexican
A former Pump Room chef cranks out gourmet entrées such as
braised leg of lamb in three sauces and skewered shrimp with
coconut at this hectic eatery in an unassuming, mini strip mall.
The wait for a table is long and reservations are not accepted, but
you can call ahead and put your name on a list. They provide
wine glasses and corkscrews. No corkage fee.
(847) 329-9810, www.whollyfrijolesgrill.com, Mon–Thurs 11–9, Fri
11–9:30, Sat 11–10, Sun closed Ⓟ

WISE GUYS $
2462 W. Armitage (Western), Logan Square
Italian/Pizza
This place has gone through a few metamorphoses in recent
years, but new management seems to have turned things around.
They've spruced up the décor and crank out a mean slice of New
York–style pizza. They provide plastic cups and corkscrews and
will put your bottles in the cooler upon request. No corkage fee.
(773) 252-7900, Mon–Thurs 4–11, Fri–Sat 4–1, Sun 12–9 Ⓟ

WRIGHTWOOD SKEWERS & CAFÉ $$
3640 W. Wrightwood (Central Park), Logan Square
Eclectic/Brunch
The menu consists entirely of skewers that reflect cuisines
from around the globe. There's an Athenian-style chicken skewer,
an Indonesian pork satay skewer, an Italian seafood skewer, and
many more. Servings are generous, and the cooking time is a
little long if you're in a hurry. Fridays and Saturdays feature live
jazz or acoustic music. They provide wine glasses and corkscrews
upon request.
(773) 342-2233, www.getskewered.com, Mon–Sat 7–2, 5–10,
Sun closed 🎌 ♫

YANG RESTAURANT $

28 E. Roosevelt (State), South Loop
Chinese

Surrounded by new condos, restaurants, even a Target, the estimable Yang's remains, located in the back of the Roosevelt Hotel just steps from the Roosevelt stop on the Red Line. They actually have a license to serve beer and wine but still allow customers to BYOB for chump change. They provide beer glasses.

(312) 986-1688, www.yangrestaurant.com, Mon–Thurs 11–9:30, Fri–Sat 11–10:30, Sun 12–9

YES THAI $

5211 N. Damen (Foster), Lincoln Square
Thai

The staff here goes the extra mile in every detail, from using all coconut milk in the tom kha, to the fresh, contemporary décor, to offering white and red wine glasses. In addition to wine glasses, they also provide pint glasses, Champagne flutes, corkscrews, and ice buckets upon request. No corkage fee.

(773) 878-3487, www.yesthaicuisine.com, Mon–Thurs 11:30–9:30, Fri–Sat 11:30–10:30, Sun 3–9, reservations recommended on weekends 🗮

ZEN NOODLES $$

1852 W. North (Wolcott), Bucktown
Pan-Asian/Sushi

This pan-Asian stir-fry place has been waiting for its liquor license for so long that they finally started serving sushi at the bar instead of alcohol. Other than doing away with the front patio, everything else from the Hi-Ricky's era (the healthy, delicious food and cute décor) is the same. They provide wine glasses, ice buckets, and corkscrews. No corkage fee.

(773) 276-8300, www.zennoodles.com, Mon–Thurs 10–10, Fri–Sat 10–11, Sun 11–10

BYOB Etiquette at Licensed Restaurants

The whole idea of allowing BYOB at licensed restaurants started as a courtesy to customers who had a distinctive bottle in their cellar and wanted to bring it for a special occasion. The increased fascination with wine expanded on this idea, and now many restaurants allow customers to bring in their own bottles on a regular basis

In the following section, I present "Restaurants That Allow BYOB for Corkage Fees of $15 or Less," a guide to a growing number of restaurants with liquor licenses that allow customers to BYOB. Accompanying this trend is the need for guidelines on how to navigate this new territory. What to tip? What to bring? What not to bring? Before you take advantage of this excellent opportunity to save money and bring something special from your own cellar, here are a few tips, gathered from restaurants in the Chicagoland area that allow this practice.

- **Order a bottle or round from the restaurant.** If you're going to bring in your own bottle of wine, perhaps order something from the bar, too, i.e., a round of cocktails or a bottle of wine from the restaurant's list.

- **Expect to pay a corkage fee.** Restaurants charge a corkage fee of anywhere from $5–$50 a bottle to uncork the bottle, decant the wine, chill it, pour it, and provide any other beverage service necessary.

- **Tip on service.** Restaurants provide the same service as though the wine were ordered from their own list (or at least, they should). Tip as though you purchased the bottle at the restaurant. This can be tricky, since you paid retail. One suggestion is to tip about 20% on the most expensive house wine on the menu.

- **Limit to one or two bottles.** Again, allowing BYOB at licensed restaurants is merely a courtesy to customers. Restaurants are happy to do this, but they usually ask you to limit it to one or two bottles.

- **Call ahead.** Understandably, some restaurants do not allow you to bring in a wine they already offer. When making your reservation, make sure that the wine you're bringing is not on the restaurant's list. If they don't have this restriction, call just to make the house aware you are bringing one in.

- **Make sure they have the proper equipment.** Many sommeliers told tales of opening up old bottles with dried-out cork. If this happens they may need a pump to get the old cork out. Phone ahead to make sure the restaurant has the proper equipment if you're bringing an old bottle of wine.

- **Don't bring in a disproportionate amount of alcohol.** One big no-no? Bringing in several magnums for a small table, or an amount of any alcohol that's disproportionate to the number of people at the table.

- **Offer a glass to the staff.** It's in good form to offer a glass to the sommelier, head chef, or waiter. They may accept it, decline it, or share it with another staff member.

- **Put your juice in the trunk.** Half-full, half-empty, it doesn't matter how you look at it. Open container laws in Illinois state that you cannot have opened bottles of alcohol in the passenger compartment of your vehicle. However, you can put your half-empty bottles in the trunk. One suggestion: grab an empty wine bottle box from a wine store, put it in your trunk, and the next time you want to take home your half-empties you can just stow them in there. Perhaps invest in a couple of bottle stoppers in case the cork doesn't reseal very well.

—J.I.

Restaurants That Allow BYOB for Corkage Fees of $15 or Less*

Although the following restaurants have a fully stocked bar and/or wine list, they allow customers to BYOB for a corkage fee of $15 or less. Personally, I am amazed that so many restaurants with liquor licenses allow BYOB—and for such a modest fee. The corkage is charged for many reasons: to compensate for the fact that customers are not ordering a bottle of wine from the restaurant; for use of stemware, decanters, and corkscrews; and for the corkage and beverage service itself. However, to attract more customers, these restaurants allow BYOB for a modest corkage.

The corkage fees listed on the following pages are charged per 750 ml bottle, unless noted otherwise. If the listing states that a restaurant only allows, for example, wine, or wine and beer, that means they do not allow hard alcohol. *Unless additional restrictions are noted, you are allowed to bring any bottle of wine you choose, even if it is on the restaurant's wine list.* If you go to a restaurant that does not allow wines on their list, call ahead to make sure your bottle is allowed, as wine lists change frequently.

This is not meant to be an exhaustive list of restaurants in this category. It does represent, however, a good cross-section of cuisines, locations, and price points. If you would like to bring a special bottle to a restaurant not on this list, simply call ahead and ask about their policy. They may charge more than $15 a bottle, or they may not allow BYOB at all. But it doesn't hurt to ask. You may be surprised.

—J.I.

*Corkage fees were current as of press time.

1776

397 Virginia St. (Route 14), Crystal Lake
Contemporary American
(815) 356-1776
Corkage: $15

ADOBO GRILL

1610 N. Wells (North), Old Town
Nuevo Latino
(773) 252-9990
Corkage: $15; none if vintage is 10 years old or more

AGAMI

4712 N. Broadway (Leland), Uptown
Sushi
(773) 506-1854
Corkage: $15; beer, wine, and sake allowed

ALT THAI

40 S. Arlington Heights Rd. (NW Hwy.), Arlington Heights
Thai
(847) 797-8442
Corkage: $10

ASADO BRAZILIAN GRILL

1012 Church (Maple), Evanston
Brazilian
(847) 425-4175
Corkage: $10

A TAVOLA

2148 W. Chicago (Leavitt), Ukrainian Village
Italian
(773) 276-7567
Corkage: $15

BARRINGTON COUNTRY BISTRO

700 W. NW Hwy. (Hart), Barrington
French
(847) 842-1300
Corkage: $15

BICE

158 E. Ontario (Michigan), Gold Coast
Italian
(312) 664-1474
Corkage: $15

BISTRO CAMPAGNE

4518 N. Lincoln (Sunnyside), Lincoln Square
French
(773) 271-6100
Corkage: $15

BISTROT MARGOT

1437 N. Wells (Schiller), Old Town
French
(312) 587-3660
Corkage: $15

BOB CHINN'S CRAB HOUSE

393 S. Milwaukee (Dundee), Wheeling
Seafood
(847) 520-3633
Corkage: $10

BRANMOR'S AMERICAN GRILL

300 S. Veterans Pkwy. (Lily Cache Ln.), Bolingbrook
American
(630) 226-9926
Corkage: $15; wines on their list not allowed

BUONA TERRA
2535 N. California (Logan Blvd.), Logan Square
Italian
(773) 289-3800
Corkage: $15

CAFÉ LE COQ
734 Lake (Oak Park Ave.), Oak Park
French
(708) 848-2233
Corkage: $15

CAFÉ LUCCI
609 Milwaukee (Central), Glenview
Italian
(847) 729-2268
Corkage: $15; wines on their list not allowed

CAFFE LA SCALA
626 S. Racine (Harrison), University Village/Little Italy
Italian
(312) 421-7262
Corkage: $10

CARLOS
429 Temple (Waukegan), Highland Park
French
(847) 432-0770
Corkage: none on Mondays; $30 otherwise

CHEF'S STATION
915 Davis (Maple), Evanston
Contemporary American
(847) 570-9821
Corkage: $15; wines on their list not allowed

CONVITO CAFE & MARKET
1515 Sheridan, Wilmette
French
(847) 251-3654
Corkage: $10

D & J BISTRO
466 S. Rand (Main), Lake Zurich
French
(847) 438-8001
Corkage: $15

DOLCE
250 Marriott Dr. (Milwaukee), Lincolnshire
Italian
(847) 478-0990
Corkage: $12

DOZIKA
601 Dempster (Chicago), Evanston
Pan-Asian/Sushi
(847) 869-9740
Corkage: $15 per bottle of wine; $1 per bottle of beer

ETHIOPIAN DIAMOND
6120 N. Broadway (Granville), Edgewater
Ethiopian
(773) 338-6100
Corkage: $1.50 per person (this is not a typo!)

EVERGREEN RESTAURANT
2411 S. Wentworth (24th), Chinatown
Chinese
(312) 225-8898
Corkage: $5

FEAST
1616 N. Damen (North), Bucktown
American/Global
(773) 772-7100
Corkage: $10; none on Mondays and Tuesdays

FRIED GREEN TOMATOES
213 N. Main St. (Perry), Galena
Italian
(815) 777-3938
Corkage: $10

GALE STREET INN
4914 N. Milwaukee (Higgins), Niles
American/Ribs
(773) 725-1300
Corkage: $10

GIO
1631 Chicago (Davis), Evanston
Italian
(847) 869-3900
Corkage: $15

GIOCO
1312 S. Wabash (13th), South Loop
Italian
(312) 939-3870
Corkage: $15

GLENN'S DINER
1820 W. Montrose (Honore), Ravenswood
Seafood
(773) 506-1720
Corkage: $5

GREEK ISLANDS
200 S. Halsted (Adams), Greek Town
Greek
(312) 782-9855
Corkage: $15

IL COVO
2152 N. Damen (Webster), Bucktown
Italian
(773) 862-5555
Corkage: $15; wines on their list not allowed

IL VICINATO
2435 S. Western (24th), Little Village
Italian
(773) 927-5444
Corkage: $15

JOE'S SEAFOOD, PRIME STEAK & STONE CRAB
60 E. Grand (Wabash), River North
Steak House
(312) 379-5637
Corkage: $15

KAZE SUSHI
2032 W. Roscoe (Damen), Roscoe Village
Sushi
(773) 327-4860
Corkage: $15; wine and sake allowed

KENDALL COLLEGE DINING ROOM
900 N. Branch St. (Chicago), River West
Contemporary American
(312) 752-2328
Corkage: $15

KITE MANDARIN AND SUSHI
3341 N. Lincoln (School), Lakeview
Chinese/Japanese/Sushi
(773) 472-2100
Corkage: $5

KOI
624 Davis (Chicago), Evanston
Chinese/Sushi
(847) 866-6969
Corkage: $10

LA PETIT AMELIA
618 Church (Chicago), Evanston
French
(847) 328-3333
Corkage: $15; wines on their list not allowed

LA PETITE FOLIE
1504 E. 55th (Lake Park Ave.), Hyde Park
French
(773) 493-1394
Corkage: $15

LA PIAZZA
410 Circle Ave. (Madison), Forest Park
Italian
(708) 366-4010
Corkage: $15

LAWRY'S THE PRIME RIB
100 E. Ontario (Rush), Near North
Steak House
(312) 787-5000
Corkage: $10

Wine Discount Center

Great Wines. Great Prices. Great Staff.
Why shop anywhere else?

Join us for in-store wine tastings every Saturday 12:00 - 4:00

At the Wine Discount Center, we are committed to offering you only the highest quality wines in all price categories at the lowest prices in town. With great wines, great prices, easy parking and a friendly, knowledgeable staff, we think that you'll agree when we boast of being Chicagoland's best wine store!

CHICAGO
1826 N. Elston
(773)489-3454

HIGHLAND PARK
1350 Old Skokie Road
(847)831-1049

FOREST PARK
Inside Famous Liquors
7714 W. Madison
(708)366-2500

BUFFALO GROVE
1170 McHenry Rd. (Rte. 83)
(847)478-0300

winediscountcenter.com

The Gourmet Grape Inc.

A Fine Wine, Gift Basket & Accessory Shoppe

Fine Wines
from
Around the World

* **Wine Club**
  (Monthly wine club with three price ranges to fit any budget ~ also makes a great gift!)

* **Third Thursday Wine Tastings**
  (On the Third Thursday of every month, we have a mix and mingle wine tasting. Check out the schedule on our website.)

* **Private Wine Tastings Customized To Fit Your Needs**
  (Schedule a private wine tasting at the store for you and your friends or a work party.)

We also specialize in
Custom Designed Gift Baskets
creating
"Distinctive Gifts for the Individual"

773.388.0942 ph
3530 N Halsted Street
www.gourmetgrape.com

provenance
food and wine

2528 n california, logan square

- boutique wines

- gourmet specialty items

- gift baskets

- fresh bread delivered daily

- available for private tastings
  and other events

773.384.0699
www.provenancefoodandwine.com

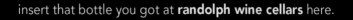

insert that bottle you got at **randolph wine cellars** here.

randolph
wine cellars we will help you find
the **perfect** bottle.

**randolph wine cellars
& the tasting room**

1415 w randolph st. | chicago, il
312.942.1212 | www.tlcwine.com

*T*THINK

**Upscale dining
and Italian-based menu
in Bucktown.**

2235 N. Western
Chicago, IL 60647
773.394.0537

www.think-cafe.com

LOVELLS OF LAKE FOREST
915 S. Waukegan (Everett), Lake Forest
Contemporary American/French
(847) 234-8013
Corkage: $15

LULA CAFÉ
2537 N. Kedzie (Wrightwood), Logan Square
Eclectic
(773) 489-9554
Corkage: $10

MAGNOLIA CAFÉ
1224 W. Wilson (Magnolia), Uptown
Contemporary American
(773) 728-8785
Corkage: $15; wines on their list not allowed

MARCHÉ
833 W. Randolph (Halsted), West Loop
French
(312) 226-8399
Corkage: $15

MAZA
2748 N. Lincoln (Diversey), Lakeview
Mediterranean
(773) 929-9600
Corkage: $7; only beer and wine allowed

MEIJI
623 W. Randolph (Jefferson), West Loop
Japanese/Sushi
(312) 887-9999
Corkage: $15; none on Mondays; wines or sakes on their list not allowed

NANA BISTRO & LOUNGE
2825 N. Lincoln (Diversey), Lakeview
Italian
(773) 281-7200
Corkage: $7

NICK'S FISHMARKET
10275 W. Higgins (Mannheim), Rosemont
Seafood
(847) 298-8200
Corkage: $15

OPERA
1301 S. Wabash (13th), South Loop
Contemporary Chinese
(312) 461-0161
Corkage: $15; wines on their list not allowed

P.S. BANGKOK
3345 N. Clark (Roscoe), Lakeview
Thai
(773) 871-7777
Corkage: $10; wines on their list not allowed

PARKERS' OCEAN GRILL
1000 31st (Highland), Downers Grove
Seafood
(630) 960-5700
Corkage: $15

THE PEPPER LOUNGE
3441 N. Sheffield (Roscoe), Lakeview
Contemporary American
(773) 665-7377
Corkage: $15; wines on their list not allowed

PHILANDER'S
Carleton of Oak Park, 1110 Pleasant, Oak Park
American/Continental
(708) 848-4250
Corkage: $15; wines on their list not allowed

PIAZZA BELLA
2116 W. Roscoe (Leavitt), Roscoe Village
Italian
(773) 477-7330
Corkage: $15; only wine allowed

PORT EDWARD RESTAURANT
20 W. Algonquin (River Rd.), Algonquin
Seafood
(847) 658-5441
Corkage: $15; wines on their list not allowed

RAW BAR
3720 N. Clark (Waveland), Lakeview
Persian/Seafood
(773) 348-7291
Corkage: $7

RED LIGHT
820 W. Randolph (Halsted), West Loop
Pan-Asian
(312) 733-8880
Corkage: $15; wines on their list not allowed

RUSSIAN TEA TIME
77 E. Adams (Michigan), Loop
Russian
(312) 360-0000
Corkage: $10

SCOOZI!
410 W. Huron (Sedgwick), River North
Italian
(312) 943-5900
Corkage: $15; wines on their list not allowed

SCYLLA
1952 N. Damen (Armitage), Bucktown
Eclectic/Seafood
(773) 227-2995
Corkage: $15; limit to one bottle; wines on their list not allowed

SHAW'S CRAB HOUSE
21 E. Hubbard (State), Near North
Seafood
(312) 527-2722
Corkage: $15

SIAM PASTA
809 Dempster (Elmwood), Evanston
Thai
(847) 328-4614
Corkage: $5

SILVER SPOON
710 N. Rush (Huron), River North
Thai
(312) 944-7100
Corkage: $2 per person

SMITH & WOLLENSKY
318 N. State (Kinzie), Near North
Steak House
(312) 670-9900
Corkage: none; wines on their list not allowed (they urge customers to tip on wine service)

SOCCA
3301 N. Clark (Aldine), Lakeview
French-Italian
(773) 248-1155
Corkage: $15 (waived if wine is brought from Que Syrah with receipt)

SQUARE KITCHEN
4600 N. Lincoln (Wilson), Lincoln Square
Contemporary American
(773) 751-1500
Corkage: $15; wines on their list not allowed

SUSHI LUXE
5201 N. Clark (Foster), Andersonville
Sushi
(773) 334-0770
Corkage: $10 on weekends; none on weekdays

LA TACHE
1475 W. Balmoral (Clark), Andersonville
French
(773) 334-7168
Corkage: $15

TANK
4514 N. Lincoln (Sunnyside), Lincoln Square
Sushi
(773) 769-2600
Corkage: $15; wines and sakes on their list not allowed

TAPAS BARCELONA
1615 Chicago (Davis), Evanston
Spanish
(847) 866-9900
Corkage: $12

THAI AROMA
941 W. Randolph (Sangamon), West Loop
Thai
(312) 492-7889
Corkage: $15

TIMO
464 N. Grand (Halsted), River West
Contemporary Italian
(312) 226-4300
Corkage: none; two bottles maximum; wines must be from your
personal cellar (otherwise you will be charged corkage; owner
uses his discretion about what's allowed and encourages patrons
to tip)

TIPARO'S
1540 N. Clark (North), Old Town
Thai
(312) 712-9900
Corkage: $7; only wine allowed

TOMBOY
5402 N. Clark (Balmoral), Andersonville
Contemporary American
(773) 907-0636
Corkage: $5 per table; only beer and wine allowed

TRATTORIA NO. 31
605 W. 31st (Wallace), Bridgeport
Italian
(312) 326-3500
Corkage: $5

TRATTORIA ROMA
1535 N. Wells (North), Old Town
Italian
(312) 644-7907
Corkage: $10; $15 if wine is on their list

TRUCCHI ITALIAN BISTRO
5141 Main (Curtiss), Downers Grove
Italian
(630) 434-7700
Corkage: $15

VA PENSIERO
1566 Oak (Davis), Evanston
Italian
(847) 475-4234
Corkage: $15

VINCI
1732 N. Halsted (Willow), Lincoln Park
Italian
(312) 266-1199
Corkage: $15; none if vintage is more than 10 years old

Off the Beaten Path BYOBs

Improv theaters? Art galleries? Restaurants aren't the only places to BYOB in Chicago. Recognizing the tremendous appeal of a BYOB policy, these venues encourage customers to bring their own.

AMBROSIA CAFÉ
1963 N. Sheffield (Armitage), Lincoln Park
Hookah Lounge
By day, this café is filled with DePaul students noshing on build-your-own sandwiches, salads, and Mediterranean eats. At night, the lights go down and the hookahs come out. Choose from 11 flavors of tobacco. They have wine glasses and ice buckets on hand and will open your bottles and keep them chilled upon request.
(773) 404-4450, www.ambrosiachicago.com, Sun–Thurs 10–1a, Fri–Sat 10–3a

CAFÉ MUD
1936 Maple (Emerson), Evanston
Café
Jazz combos and pianists liven up this cute café from a small, elevated stage while customers sip espresso or fuss over the Sunday crossword. They usually feature jazz performances on Thursday nights and pianists on Sunday afternoons. Check the Web site for a performance schedule.
(847) 733-9904, www.cafemud.com, Mon–Thurs 8–10:30, Fri–Sun 10–10:30

CORNSERVATORY
4210 N. Lincoln (Berteau), North Center
Improv Theater
The brainchild of Robert Bouwman and Todd Schaner, this offbeat theater company offers late-night productions and the long-running show "Floss!" a part-dance, part-comic parody on Saturday nights at 8. Wednesday night performances are only $7 (add BYOB to the mix and you have one cheap date). Other Corn Productions, mostly sketch comedies, are held on Thursdays at 8 and Fridays and Saturdays at 8 and 10 or 11. Cornservatory is a League of Chicago Theater member, so you may find last-minute half-price tickets at Hot Tix.
(312) 409-6435, www.cornservatory.org

CREATE JEWELRY STUDIO
1400 N. Milwaukee (Wolcott), Wicker Park
Jewelry Studio
This open-space studio lets customers create their own jewelry, using semiprecious stones, Swarovski crystals, and other materials, with the help of talented staff. Create is available after normal business hours (listed below) for a girls' night out, bachelorette party, wine tasting, or any other private event. They encourage you to bring your own sangria, wine and cheese, or whatever floats your boat. There is a five-person minimum, and the hourly rates are extremely reasonable.
(773) 252-1543, www.createstudiochicago.com, Mon closed, Tues–Sat 11–6, Sun 12–6

F212
401 N. Wells (Kinzie), River North
Café/Lounge
Sometimes you just want to chill after dinner and have dessert in a loungey atmosphere with your own bottle of wine instead of a crowded, noisy bar. F212 is the place. They have a long list of decadent chocolate desserts (raspberry white chocolate cake, chocolate hazelnut mousse, chocolate "sushi") that will go perfectly with that bottle of Prosecco. DJs provide entertainment Wednesday through Saturday nights. They provide wine glasses and pint glasses and will put your bottles in the cooler upon request.
(312) 670-4212, www.f212lounge.com, Mon–Fri 8–12, Sat 10–12, Sun 10–5

GUESS HOOKAH
1829 W. Chicago (Wood), East Ukrainian Village
Hookah Lounge

If there is a hookah hangout for the college crowd, this place is it. After surveying the storefront of tobaccos, hookahs, and accessories, drift into the lounge, where comfy couches, exposed brick, skylights, and over 100 flavors of tobacco await. On Sunday nights the lounge features DJs or live music. They provide stemware for wine and plastic cups for beer. No food is served, but soda is available.
(773) 486-9522, www.guesshookah.com, Mon–Thurs 12–12, Fri–Sat 12–2, Sun 3–11

HOUSE OF HOOKAH
607 W. Belmont (Broadway), Lakeview
Hookah Lounge

Flop down on a cushy pillow and float away in a plume of smoke at this hookah haven in Lakeview. There are over 70 flavors of tobacco to choose from, and if you don't wish to indulge in a spinach pie or other available treats, you can even bring your own food (wow) for a $1-per-person fee. They have some plastic and paper cups and a corkscrew or two on hand; the rest is up to you.
(773) 348-1550, www.chicagohookah.com, Mon–Tues 7–12, Wed–Thurs 7–1, Fri–Sat 4–3, Sun closed

MUSE CAFÉ
817 N. Milwaukee (Chicago), River West
Café/Gallery

This is a combined coffeehouse, art gallery, free wi-fi hot spot, and jazz and electronic music venue. Muse hosts the monthly Electro-Acoustic Workshop and Jazztronic Experiment, an improv-based workshop in which DJ Don Solo directs instrumentalists to drop in and out while he provides programmed backbeats. You can book Muse for after-hours parties (they provide the food) for up to 60 people and bring your own wine, beer, etc. They also offer bimonthly poetry nights, live jazz, and gallery openings. Check their Web site for a schedule.
(312) 850-2233, www.musecafechicago.com, Mon–Fri 8–8, Sat 10–6, Sun closed

PH PRODUCTIONS
3408 N. Sheffield (Roscoe), Lakeview
Improv Theater

This small improv production company produces shows three nights a week at the Stage Left Theater. Fridays and Saturdays offer an interactive improv show at 11 and "pHrenzy," a late-night hyperactive game show, at 12:30. There are also shows on Thursday nights, and all performances allow BYOB. Check the Web site for details.
(773) 490-1360, www.whatisph.com

THE PLAYGROUND IMPROV THEATER
3209 N. Halsted (Belmont), Lakeview
Improv Theater

This long-standing improv company, in the old ComedySportz space, features seasoned troupes who riff off of audience suggestions and perform sketch comedy. There are three long-running, open-run shows: "Big Yellow Bus" on Thursdays at 8; "Graffiti" on Fridays at 10; and "Don't Spit the Water," a manic game show, at 10:30. There are also midnight shows on Fridays and Saturdays and other improv performances every night of the week. Tickets are approximately $5–$12. Call the box office for show times.
(773) 871-3793, www.theplayground.com

RITZ TANGO CAFÉ
933 N. Ashland (Augusta), Noble Square
Café/Dance Studio

Here, you can have your tango and your Tempranillo, too. This café serves coffee and sandwiches during the day, but at night the baristas clear the hardwood floors for tango dance lessons. Dancers mingle and sip on their own wine afterward (the restaurant has wine glasses on hand). It may be the most Cinderella-like transformation of any coffeehouse.
(773) 235-2233, www.ritztangocafe.com, Mon 9–12, Tues, Thurs 9–12, Fri 9:30–11:30, Sat 2–5, Sun 11–2, 6–10 (hours are for dancing only)

Wine & Spirits Stores

CHICAGO

Wine & Spirits Stores A–Z

AVONDALE'S
3018 N. Milwaukee (Wellington), Logan Square
This neighborhood liquor store is known for its extensive Eastern European beer and vodka selections. Two aisles are packed with mostly Polish and other imported beers, and one entire wall is stocked with vodkas from all over the world. Most of the wines are from California, Australia, and Italy and average about $10 a bottle.
(773) 227-1793, www.avondalebeverages.com, Mon–Fri 9–10, Sat 8:30–10, Sun 11–9

BIN 36
339 N. Dearborn (Kinzie), River North
Bin 36's retail store sells bottles of the same 50 or so wines offered by the glass in their restaurant, most for under $20. Wine director Brian Duncan works with winemakers to produce "Brian's Blend" wines exclusively for Bin 36. You can also order wine and accessories from their Web site and at their Wicker Park and Lincolnshire locations.
(312) 755-9463, www.bin36.com, Mon–Sat 10–12, Sun 12–11

BINNY'S BEVERAGE DEPOT
Hundreds of wines, beers, and spirits await at Binny's 18 Chicagoland locations. Each store has different features, such as wine cellars, wine storage, wine tastings, classes, gourmet grocery items, walk-in humidors, and cigar selections. Every week they conduct special events and tastings, from seminars on premium whiskies to American wine tastings to an annual Scotch tasting. Shop online, then pick up your order when it's ready at your favorite location. You can also go online and access a list of wines rated 90 points or better by *Wine Spectator*, *The Wine Advocate*, and *International Wine Cellar*. Call each location for hours.
www.binnys.com

(continued on next page)

BINNY'S BEVERAGE DEPOT (cont'd)

Chicago

213 W. Grand (Wells), River North, (312) 332-0012

3000 N. Clark (Wellington), Lakeview (Ivanhoe Castle & Catacombs Tasting Room), (773) 935-9400

1531 E. 53rd St. (Lake Park Ave.), Hyde Park, (773) 324-5000

Suburbs

124 McHenry Rd. (Lake Cook and 83), Buffalo Grove, (847) 459-2200

767 W. Golf (Market Place Shopping Center), Des Plaines, (847) 956-1000

7330 W. North (Harlem), Elmwood Park, (708) 456-2112

670 Roosevelt Rd. (Pickwick Place Shopping Center), Glen Ellyn, (630) 545-2550

71 N. Greenbay Rd. (Hubbard Woods Shopping Center), Glencoe, (847) 835-3900

153 Skokie Valley Hwy. (Cross Roads Shopping Center), Highland Park, (847) 831-5400

4610 W. Elm (on Route 120), McHenry, (815) 385-3200

790 Royal St. George (Cress Creek Square Shopping Center), Naperville, (630) 717-0100

8935 N. Milwaukee (Dempster), Niles, (847) 966-2300

103A Orland Park Pl. (151st), Orland Park, (708) 226-9902

3121 Thatcher (Belmont), River Grove, (708) 456-7400

323 W. Golf (Roselle), Schaumburg, (847) 882-6000

5100 W. Dempster (Gross Point Rd.), Skokie, (847) 674-4200

1950 Lincoln Hwy. (Randall), St. Charles, (630) 377-1671

6920 S. Route 83 (Plainfield Rd.), Willowbrook, (630) 654-0988

CABERNET & CO.
732 Lake (Oak Park Ave.), Oak Park
Here you'll find a whittled-down, thoughtful selection of domestic and imported wines at reasonable price points. The frequent tastings and convenient location in charming downtown Oak Park make this an attractive spot. Complimentary tastings are Fridays 5–7, Saturdays 1–7, and Sundays 12–4.
(708) 763-9463, Mon 2–7, Tues–Wed 10–7, Thurs 10–8, Fri–Sat 10–7, Sun 12–4

CONVITO CAFE & MARKET
1515 Sheridan (Plaza del Lago), Wilmette
The operative word here is Italian: red, white, dessert, and sparkling wines from nearly every one of Italy's regions. Pluck a bottle or two and take it across the way to the full-service restaurant for no corkage.
(847) 251-3654, www.convitoitaliano.com, Mon–Fri 10–6:30, Sat 9:30–6, Sun 11:30–5

EATZI'S
2828 N. Clark (Diversey), Lakeview
Whether you're looking for Yellowtail or Silver Oak, domestic or imported, you'll find the wine you need at this gourmet grocery, located at basement level in the Century Shopping Center (beer selection, however, is slim).
(773) 832-9063, www.eatzis.com, Sun–Thurs 10–9, Fri–Sat 10–10

FINE WINE BROKERS
4621 N. Lincoln (Wilson), Lincoln Square
This European-style wine shop in now-trendy but still charming Lincoln Square carries wines from artisans around the world. They also specialize in organic selections from small estates in France, Italy, Spain, Australia, and the U.S.
(773) 989-8166, www.fwbchicago.com, Mon–Fri 12–7:30, Sat 10–6:30, Sun 12–4

FOODSTUFFS
2106 Central (Hartley), Evanston
338 Park (Green Bay Rd.), Glencoe
255 Westminster Rd. (Western), Lake Forest
1456 Waukegan (Lake), Glenview
Foodstuffs has expanded from a small catering and cooking demonstration company in 1979 to a full-fledged gourmet prepared food and grocery business, with four North Shore locations. Only the Glencoe and Lake Forest stores carry wine—mostly boutique, domestic, limited-production bottles in the $12–$40 range.
(847) 328-7704 (Evanston); (847) 835-5105 (Glencoe); (847) 234-6600 (Lake Forest); (847) 832-9999 (Glenview); Mon–Fri 10–6:30, Sat 9–5, Sun 10–5 (all locations); www.foodstuffs.com

FOREMOST LIQUORS
1040 W. Argyle (Broadway), Uptown
Not only is Foremost a convenient place to stop, being in the midst of several Asian BYOBs, but they also carry a surprisingly good selection of boutique wines and imported beers. Here you'll find "33," the Vietnamese export, as well as "Tiger," a Singapore brew just released after a 10-year hiatus.
(773) 989-0808, Mon–Sat 9:30–10, Sun 11:30–8

FOX & OBEL FOOD MARKET
401 E. Illinois (McClurg), Streeterville
If you can make it past the tempting cases of freshly baked breads and pastries, seafood, prepared gourmet foods, and other goodies flowing from the shelves, you'll find a wide selection of fine wine, sake, beer, and spirits tucked away in the back of the store.
(312) 410-7301, www.foxandobel.com, 7–9 every day

GALLERIA LIQUEURS
1559 N. Wells (North), Old Town
Where else can you find a bottle of Taittinger at midnight? Owner Ben Pourkhalili offers 100 boutique and smaller-production wines under $12 as well as wine accessories, gift bags, high-end wines, microbrews, and premium spirits. Complimentary tastings every Saturday from 3–6.
(312) 867-7070, Mon–Thurs 9–12, Fri–Sat 9–1a

THE GODDESS & GROCER
1646 N. Damen (North), Bucktown
25 E. Delaware (State), Gold Coast
This gourmet grocery's compact size, convenient loading zone, and thoughtful selection means you're in and out in about five minutes, always with a terrific bottle of boutique wine. Owner Debbie Sharpe also stocks a cooler of can't-miss bottles of chilled whites, sparkling wines, and beers.
(773) 342-3200, Mon–Fri 11–9, Sat 10–8, Sun 10–7 (Bucktown);
(312) 896-2600, 7–9 every day (Gold Coast);
www.goddessandgrocer.com

THE GOURMET GRAPE
3530 N. Halsted (Addison), Lakeview
This beautiful, high-end store offers boutique wines, a large selection of gifts and accessories, and first-class service (and, sometimes, music streaming from the grand piano). A great place to pick up fine glassware if you're heading to a BYOB that has none. Complimentary tastings every Saturday afternoon.
(773) 388-0942, www.gourmetgrape.com, Mon–Sat 11–9,
Sun 12–6

HOUSE OF GLUNZ
1206 N. Wells (Division), Old Town
In 1888 Louis Glunz arrived from Germany and opened what is now an Old Town institution. Four generations later, House of Glunz is still family owned and operated. They offer Old and New World wines; microbrews from Belgium, U.S., and Germany; and glassware, corkscrews, and other accessories. Pull into the loading zone and pick up a preordered bottle on your way to a BYOB. Complimentary tastings every Saturday from 3–6 (the European-style tasting room in back is something to experience).
(312) 642-3000, www.houseofglunz.com, Mon–Fri 9–8, Sat 10–7,
Sun 2–5

IN FINE SPIRITS
5418 N. Clark (Balmoral), Andersonville
Husband-and-wife team Shane and Jill Kissack opened up this
beautiful shop in 2005, much to the delight of the growing
neighborhood, where a bottle of boutique wine was hard to find.
The selection is organized by varietal, but if you aren't sure what
you're looking for, help is always there. They also sell premium
sakes for the sushi BYOBs nearby, as well as microbrews, stemware, BYOB gift baskets, and other goodies. Complimentary
tastings every other Saturday from 3–6; check the Web site for
other events.
(773) 506-9463, www.infinespirits.com, Mon closed, Tues–Fri
12–8, Sat 11–7, Sun 12–6

JUICY WINE COMPANY
694 N. Milwaukee (Huron), River West
Rodney Alex, former owner of Taste wine store in Wicker Park,
has resurfaced in the old Iggy's space with this retail/lounge
hybrid. Alex will offer the same ingredients that made Taste so
unique: a relaxed vibe, rare cheeses, and boutique wines. The first
floor is a retail store and the second floor features a lounge, cozy
booths, and a DJ for late-night swirling. Call for hours.
(312) 482-6620, www.juicywine.com

JUST GRAPES
560 W. Washington (Clinton), West Loop
The focus here is on small, artisanal producers from all over the
world. And if you'd like to try before you buy, Just Grapes has a
self-serve automated tasting bar, one of only a few in the U.S. You
first purchase a "smart card," then dispense and taste any of 24
wines. The value gets deducted from the card. Complimentary
tastings every Saturday from 1–4.
(312) 627-9463, www.justgrapes.net, Mon–Thurs 8–7, Fri 8–8, Sat
12–6, Sun closed

KAFKA WINE CO.
3325 N. Halsted (Buckingham), Lakeview
The wines here are organized by tasting profile—toasty, spicy, fruity, earthy, or floral/herbal—90 percent of them under $15. Also choose from the "splurge" table, filled with bottles for special occasions or collectors. The fun, knowledgeable staff will never steer you to a bum bottle.
(773) 975-9463, www.kafkawine.com, Mon–Sat 12–10, Sun 12–7

KENSINGTON FINE WINES
465 E. Illinois (Lake Shore Dr.), Streeterville
Known for its wine auction house, Kensington also sells rare and fine wines at this retail store, which is down the street from Navy Pier. They carry hundreds of wines from $5–$500, though most are rare wines targeted to collectors. Tastings every Saturday from 12–4.
(312) 836-7855, www.kensingtonsfinewine.com, Mon–Sat 11–7, Sun closed

KNIGHTSBRIDGE WINE SHOPPE
824 Sunset Ridge (Skokie Blvd.), Northbrook
Tucked away behind the noisy Edens Expressway and the Skokie Blvd./Dundee intersection is this elegant boutique shop. The selection is focused on Bordeaux and Burgundy wines. There's an extensive assortment of Champagne/sparkling wines, ports, and half-bottles as well. You'll also find one of the most comprehensive wine-related book selections around. Knightsbridge has been voted one of the most beautiful wine shops in the U.S.; one step inside and you'll see why.
(847) 498-9300, www.knightsbridgewine.biz, Mon–Fri 10–7, Sat 10–6, Sun closed

LUSH WINE AND SPIRITS

1306 S. Halsted (Roosevelt), University Village
2232 W. Roscoe (Oakley), Roscoe Village

Lush is the latest offspring of Mitch and Cliff Einhorn, owners of Twisted Spoke restaurants. In addition to an incredible selection of boutique wines, Lush stocks hard-to-find bourbons and other unusual finds. Belly up to the tasting bar, where 12 to 24 bottles of wine are open every day. Or, pop in on Sundays from 2–5 for more focused tastings (they're also complimentary). They'll keep your purchase history on the computer for future purchases (gotta love that).

(312) 738-1900, www.lushwineandspirits.com, 12–10 every day (both locations)

OLIVIA'S MARKET

2014 W. Wabansia (Damen), Bucktown

This subterranean gourmet grocery carries a global selection of wine, most in the under-$20 range. They also carry sake, premium beers, chilled sparkling wine, and half-bottles. Loading zones out front make your stop more convenient in congested Bucktown.

(773) 227-4220, Mon–Fri 9–9, Sat 9–8, Sun 10–7

PASTORAL

2945 N. Broadway (Oakdale), Lakeview

This quaint, European-style shop specializes in artisan-made cheeses, breads, and wines. Their small selection of small-batch wines is designed to pair with the cheeses they carry on a daily basis, so they're ready-to-drink and "food-friendly."

(773) 472-4781, www.pastoralartisan.com, Mon closed, Tues–Fri 11–8, Sat 11–7, Sun 11–6

PRINTER'S ROW WINE SHOP

719 S. Dearborn (Polk), South Loop

Owner Flavio Gentile transformed an old pharmacy into this gorgeous wine shop. The store features rare, hard-to-find wines, premium beers, and a wide selection of glassware. Gentile will let customers taste any bottle from the middle aisle. Complimentary tastings every Friday.

(312) 663-9314, www.printersrowwine.com, Mon–Wed 11–10, Thurs–Sat 11–11, Sun 2–9

PROVENANCE FOOD AND WINE
2528 N. California (Logan Blvd.), Logan Square

Tracy Kellner's new boutique wine store is a very welcome addition to this burgeoning but previously wine-deprived neighborhood. Kellner focuses on smaller-production, boutique, food-friendly wines. The cozy but uncluttered shop also offers a limited selection of mostly domestic, handmade cheeses; Red Hen bread; meats; and other specialty foods. Free tastings every Saturday from 3–5 and a "10 under $10" table are two more reasons to stop by. (773) 384-0699, www.provenancefoodandwine.com, Mon closed, Tues–Sat 12–9, Sun 12–7

QUE SYRAH
3726 N. Southport (Grace), Lakeview

The helpful staff at this elegant shop will guide you to mostly Italian, French, and American boutique wines that range from $6–$175 a bottle. They also hold regular classes and tastings for all levels and tastes. Check the Web site for complimentary tastings and other events.
(773) 871-8888, www.quesyrahwine.com, Mon 11–8, Tues–Sat 11–9, Sun 12–7

RANDOLPH WINE CELLARS
1415 W. Randolph (Ogden), West Loop

The extremely knowledgeable staff (including professional wine judges and several sommeliers) successfully caters to novices and connoisseurs alike. They'll help you make selections from dozens of valuable and interesting wines—all without any 'tude. Complimentary, focused tastings every Saturday from 12–6.
(312) 942-1212, www.tlcwine.com, Mon–Fri 11–8, Sat 10–8, Sun 1–6

SAM'S WINE & SPIRITS

1720 N. Marcey (Willow), Lincoln Park
2010 Butterfield Rd. (Lloyd), Downers Grove
1919 Skokie Valley Rd., Highland Park

Wine Enthusiast calls Sam's "a veritable cultural center for wine." There are classes on wine and spirits (Sam's Academy), seminars, tastings, dinners, an extensive book and accessories selection, gourmet grocery, cheese shop… And if over 5,000 wines don't merit the word "superstore," then what does? Since it opened as a tavern in 1945, the family-owned and operated Sam's Wine has turned into the largest independent beverage retailer in the country. The flagship Lincoln Park store's wines (grouped by region) are literally stocked to the rafters, and the beer and spirits selections are second-to-none, making it fun to browse and discover new finds. Tasting stations around the store (on weekends) mean you can try before you buy. And it's rare to stand still for more than a minute without at least one employee popping up and asking if you need help. They now have two suburban locations: Downers Grove and Highland Park. The Downers Grove location is a somewhat whittled-down version of Sam's Lincoln Park, with the same merchandising and selections. The recently opened Highland Park store boasts a wine lounge, so you can rest your weary bones after some serious shopping. Heck, you can even open and sample a bottle just purchased at the store.
(312) 664-4394, Mon–Sat 8–9, Sun 11–6 (Lincoln Park);
(630) 705-9463, Mon–Sat 9–9, Sun 12–7 (Downers Grove);
(847) 433-9463, Mon–Sat 9–9, Sun 11–6 (Highland Park);
www.samswine.com

SANDBURG WINE CELLAR

1525 N. Clark (North), Old Town

Upstairs you'll find a selection of mass-produced wines; downstairs are about 800 rare, esoteric, boutique wines from all over the world ranging from $7–$700 a bottle. Also find microbrews and imported and domestic beers. Parking is free with purchase of $20.
(312) 337-7537, Mon–Sat 9:30–10, Sun 11–9

SCHAEFER'S
9965 Gross Point Rd. (Old Orchard), Skokie

Many of the wines here are tagged as "favorites" by staff, so after a while you can select wines favored by someone with compatible taste (an effective technique practiced by many independent bookstores). There is a wide variety of tastings and classes to take advantage of at this family-owned institution (opened as a tavern in 1936), as well as a popular wine club. The service here is incredible; staff will track down a bottle and order it for you even if it's not something in stock.

(847) 631-5711, www.schaefers.com, Mon–Wed 9–7, Thurs–Sat 9–8, Sun 11–5

SOUTHPORT GROCERY
3552 N. Southport (Addison), Lakeview

Purchase a bottle from the small gourmet grocery store here and take it to the café for brunch, lunch, or dinner without paying any corkage. Such a deal. They carry a small but interesting variety of mostly New World wines ranging from $15–$30 a bottle, a few microbrews, and sparkling wine.

(773) 665-0100, www.southportgrocery.com, Mon–Fri 8–7, Sat 8–5, Sun 8–3

A TASTE OF VINO
24 W. Chicago (Washington), Hinsdale

Owner Tanya Hart draws from her several years in the wine industry to select global wines, mostly in the under-$20 range, for this boutique shop. The wines are organized by styles, not varietal or region. For example, browse "big, bold, rich" or "smooth, luscious, juicy" wines—a great way to find new wines that suit your palate. There's also an in-store wine bar, where you can sit and enjoy wines by the glass or red or white flights.

(630) 325-8466, www.atasteofvino.com, Mon–Wed 10–7:30, Thurs–Sat 10–10, Sun closed (except November and December)

TROTTER'S TO GO
1337 W. Fullerton (Southport), Lincoln Park
Though known for its prepared gourmet food, Trotter's to Go also stocks a selection of fine domestic and imported wines. You'll find boutique, hard-to-find buys from around the world, including a good number of bottles from Oregon and Washington State. Trotter's is somewhat on the pricey side, but if you need to find a high-quality bottle of wine in a hurry (they have a parking lot, a major plus in congested Lincoln Park), then this is your place.
(773) 868-6510, www.trotterstogo.com, Mon–Sat 11–8, Sun 11–6

TUSCAN MARKET AND SHOP
141 W. Wing (Vail), Arlington Heights
It was only a matter of time before a fine wine shop opened up in the ever-expanding Arlington Heights. While primarily an Italian grocery and deli (they serve up thin-crust pizzas, pastas, sub sandwiches, and panini), Tuscan Market also carries a discerning selection of mostly boutique wines.
(847) 392-9700, www.tuscanwineshop.com, Mon–Sat 10–7, Sun closed

UNCORK IT!
393 E. Illinois (McClurg), Streeterville
The well-organized aisles of wines, beers, spirits, and food items reflect the owners' background in grocery stores (Marketplace). They carry hundreds of both boutique and mass-produced wines and spirits, a reasonably priced selection of microbrews and imported and domestic beer—plus a selection of gourmet groceries and snacks. There's free parking in the lot just west of the store with a $30 purchase.
(312) 321-9400, www.uncorkitchicago.com, Mon–Thurs 8–10:30, Fri–Sat 8–11:30, Sun 11–10

WEST LAKEVIEW LIQUORS
2156 W. Addison (Leavitt), North Center
What looks like an unassuming neighborhood liquor store is actually a fine wine and spirits haven, with great finds tucked into a small space. There are over 200 wines from 16 countries, many of them under $12. Beer tastings are every Friday from 6–9; wine or spirits tastings are every Saturday from 6–9.
(773) 525-1916, www.westlakeviewliquors.com, Mon–Thurs 10–10, Fri–Sat 10–11, Sun 11–10

WINE DISCOUNT CENTER

1826 N. Elston (Cortland), Bucktown
1170 McHenry Rd. (Weiland), Buffalo Grove
1350 Old Skokie Rd. (Old Deerfield), Highland Park
7714 W. Madison (Des Plaines Ave.), Forest Park

Bare bones décor (wines are usually displayed in their shipping boxes) and geographically challenged locations translate to incredibly great deals. But they don't skimp on quality, service, or selection here. There are wines in all price points, for neophytes to collectors, some rated by staff who use the same 100-point rating system as *Wine Spectator* and *The Wine Advocate*. Helpful, friendly staff are always on hand to help you find new favorites. Plus, complimentary tastings every Saturday from 12–4 will steer you to a great bottle for that night's BYOB.

(773) 489-3454, Mon–Fri 10–7, Sat 9–5, Sun 12–5 (Bucktown);
(847) 478-0300, Mon–Fri 10–7, Sat 9–5, Sun 12–5 (Buffalo Grove);
(847) 831-1049, Mon–Fri 10–7, Sat 9–5, Sun 12–5 (Highland Park);
(708) 366-2500, Mon–Sat 9–9, Sun 10–6 (Forest Park);
www.winediscountcenter.com

Features

Sake 101

by Larry Mechanic

What is sake? This is the most frequently asked question about sake. Is it rice wine? Is it more similar to beer? The simple answer is that sake is sake. It is made from rice, water, yeast, and a mold called "koji." It's neither wine nor beer, but sake is made using fermentation methods similar to both.

Junmai and Honjozo

Sake is similar to wine and beer in that sake has different classifications, styles, and types. The two major classifications that all sakes fall into are Junmai and Honjozo. "Junmai" literally translates into "pure rice" and is brewed in the older, more traditional method. Junmai sake can only contain four ingredients: rice, water, yeast, and koji. Junmai sakes are richer and fuller bodied than Honjozos. When looking at bottles at the store, a Junmai sake will always be labeled as such. When Junmai doesn't appear on the label, the sake generally is a Honjozo.

Ginjo and Daiginjo

The other major designations to look for on sake labels are Ginjo and Daiginjo. These classifications reflect the percentage of the rice kernel's outer hull that's milled away during the brewing process. To understand this better, it is important to know that sake is not made with the table rice we're all familiar with. The type of kernel used contains many impurities that result in poorly flavored, low-quality sake.

To be classified a Junmai or Honjozo, at least 30% of the outer hull of the kernel must be milled away. Ginjo sake must have a minimum of 40% of the hull milled away; Daiginjos must have at least 50%. Ginjo and Daiginjo reflect the pinnacle of a sake brewer's art and are best served with such delicate Japanese cuisine as sushi and sashimi.

Sake Styles

Also like wine, beer, and spirits, sake comes in many different styles:

- **Nigori:** the cloudy sake. This is the way sake has been brewed in Japan for much of its 2,000-year history. It's coarsely filtered and sweeter than most sakes. Many people enjoy its nut-like quality. It pairs well with spicy foods such as Thai and Korean cuisine.

- **Nama:** this is unpasteurized sake. "Nama" means "new" and is enjoyed by many in Japan during the summer months for its young and vibrant flavors.

- **Taru:** these are aged in cedar casks. This imparts a crisp, spicy character to the sake. Taru sake lends itself well to Asian meat dishes and to foods with bold flavors.

- **Genshu:** sake that is full strength ("genshu" means "cask strength"). All sake is fermented at 20% alcohol and most have distilled water added to lower the alcohol content to 14%–16%. Genshu sake is very full bodied/flavored and should be paired with dishes that are similarly robust in nature.

- **Specialty sakes:** this category includes sparkling sake, aged sake, flavored sake, and low-alcohol dessert sake. Some of these are novelty items and some are serious variations of mainstream premium sake.

Armed with the above information, you should be better able to understand the different styles and types of sake as well as read the various labels. Here are a few more tips for selecting a bottle of sake that's right for you:

- **Ask for assistance.** Someone in the store tasted and selected these sakes. They should be able to describe the different classifications, styles, and flavor profiles of the products on their shelves.

- **Look for a production date.** Sake should be consumed, not aged. Except for some special varieties, sake doesn't age the way that wine does. Think beer; drink it fresh.

- **Imported versus domestic.** Although a gross generalization, this is similar to comparing microbrewed and mass-produced beer, respectively. Eighty percent of sake is added water. Like beer, the source and quality of that water, in part, determines the quality of the final product. Domestic producers can import the rice, yeast, and koji, but they can't import the water.

- **Warmed or chilled?** Warming sake has been common in this country, mostly due to the poor-quality sake that used to be more prevalent. You wouldn't warm up a glass of a big Zinfandel with an alcohol content of 16%. With this in mind, imported premium sake should be chilled. Warming brings out the alcohol flavor and smothers the more subtle and delicate flavors that are the hallmark of premium sake.

- **How much does a good bottle of sake cost?** There's a much greater correlation between the cost and quality of sake than wine. Presently, there are no ratings that distort the price of sake. With sake you get what you pay for. The higher the quality the more it will cost.

The next time you're thinking about enjoying an Asian BYOB, think about picking up a bottle of sake—the drink this food was made to be enjoyed with. A word of caution, however: as the paths in Japanese gardens are never straight (an ancient Japanese belief is that bad spirits can't travel in crooked paths) so it is with sake. There are exceptions and variations to these guidelines. There is however, great delight in exploring and finding out what you enjoy when it comes to this ancient and unique beverage. Enjoy the journey.

Kanpai!

Larry Mechanic is the sake consultant at Sam's Wine & Spirits in Lincoln Park

10 Questions to Ask at Your Local Wine Shop

by Joe Kafka

You're at the wine store, but you have absolutely no idea what to look for, or what to ask. Relax. No one loves and appreciates good wine like the staff at a reputable wine shop. They're there to answer your questions, help you with food pairing, and most importantly, show you something new and exciting to try. Following are the top 10 questions we get asked at KAFKA wine co. every day. Use these questions as a guide the next time you're in a wine shop to open a dialogue with the staff and get you started on the road to fabulous new finds.

1. What wine goes with the food we're eating tonight?

This is the question we hear most often, and for good reason, because getting the correct wine and food pairing is essential. The idea is to pair flavors that enhance, not dominate, each other. Your wine merchant should be able to suggest a wine that will match in body, complement (or contrast) the flavors in your food, and still appeal to your personal taste.

2. How should this wine be served?

The way a wine is served can have a drastic influence on its flavor. As a rule, reds should be served a little below room temperature (about 55–60°F) and whites should be chilled then served after they've been out of the fridge for a few minutes. A red that's served too warm will taste too high in alcohol, and its fruit flavors will seem diminished. With a white that's served too cold, you won't taste its subtle nuances. The shape and size of the glass also have a big influence, as they affect smell. Taste is 80% smell, so be sure to get a glass that you can get your nose deep into. Most BYOBs don't carry fine stemware, so picking up a few glasses isn't a bad idea.

3. Can you help me decipher this wine label?
Wine labels contain crucial information such as the region the wine comes from; the vintage, or year when the grapes were harvested; the varietal, or grape(s) the wine is made from; and other facts. Ask the clerk to explain and clarify everything on that label that you don't understand.

4. Was this a good year?
Ask the clerk if the year on the bottle was a good growing year—one with weather favorable to the types of grapes grown in a region. This can be an indicator of what's in the bottle. On the flipside, if a certain year was an absolute disaster in a certain region, such as heavy flooding or damaging hail during harvest, your local wine store shouldn't have any of these wines on their shelves.

5. What are some of your personal favorites? Or Which are your bestsellers?
I love when someone decides to take a risk and lets me suggest my favorite wine du jour. It usually means that the customer would like to try something entirely new and that they're looking for a valuable piece of "insider information." It's also okay to play it safe and ask for something everyone seems to enjoy by asking for a crowd pleaser or a bestseller. That way you'll end up with a bottle that everyone will enjoy when you open it at your favorite BYOB.

6. I like a certain type of wine but want to try something new. Which ones would I like?
Use one of your favorite wines as a springboard to try something new. For example, tell your new best friend at the wine shop that you love Pinot Grigio but you'd like to try a different wine with a similar flavor profile. They may lead you to a Sauvignon Blanc or Albariño to satisfy your fruity white wine cravings. They're similar…but not the same.

7. Can you show me a wine that has great value for the money?

This is my favorite question. Nothing is more exciting than finding a $15 bottle of wine that tastes like a $30 or $40 bottle. It's a thrill! We wine geeks at KAFKA are completely value driven and love to share this information with our customers. You probably won't get a wine that's familiar to you; in fact, it's likely you'll be handed a bottle that's completely obscure. Do yourself a favor and trust the recommendation. You'll probably love it, and so will your wallet.

8. Do you ever have wine tastings?

Tasting is the only way to really get to know wine. Taste as much and as often as you can, I always say. Any reputable wine shop should offer a regular tasting schedule and you'd be a fool to pass it up. This way, you can sample many different wines, usually with a common theme. This is helpful in shaping and expanding your palate. Plus it's a lot of fun!

9. Do you have anything interesting or different that I should try?

Feeling adventurous? Go out on a limb! Ask for a wine with a strange name too complicated to pronounce or from some far-off land you've only dreamt of. Trying something off the radar screen is a guaranteed way to expand your palate and expose yourself to fun, new wines.

10. Are there any wines here that will last for several days?

Maybe a 7 a.m. conference call requires you to limit yourself to "just one glass" on a particular evening. Certain wines have greater longevity than others once opened. Some wines, usually reds, taste even better a day or two (or even three) after being opened. There are also delicate white wines that will only taste good the night they're opened; after that, they may as well be poured down the drain. You shouldn't have to do the guesswork. Just ask your favorite wine god and you shall receive your answer.

Now that you've got some questions to start with, run on down to the wine shop! We're waiting for you...

Joe Kafka is the proprietor of KAFKA wine co.

Wine Labels Decoded

What All That Wine Gibberish Really Means

by Mark Child

It seemed fair. You drew straws, but you wound up with the short one and now have the assignment of buying the wine for tonight's dinner.

There are a bazillion wines to choose from, and your only clues as to what might be inside any given bottle are written on the label in some foreign language—not simply French or Italian, but Wine-French or Wine-Italian. Even in English, there's wine jargon to contend with.

What does all that gibberish on a wine label mean?

Quite a bit, actually, and with a bit of practice you'll have this new language down as cold as a bottle of Champagne.

Not Just a Good Idea, It's the Law

First things first: labels are legal statements. They give you the who, what, where, when, and, sometimes, how of wine. A label is a form of consumer protection; it vouches for the authenticity of a product (but not necessarily its quality). Like any legal document, wine labels vary from place to place, reflecting the culture and society they serve. But they all have some things in common, so mastering the following two should help the next time you shop for wine.

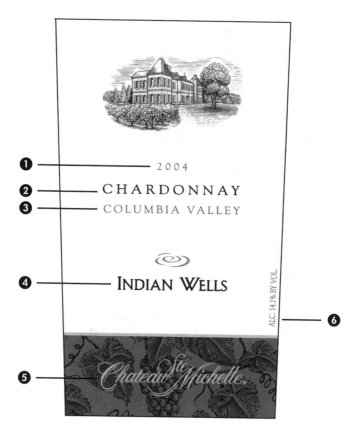

Domestic Labels

Let's start with a domestic wine. Take this bottle right here, the Chateau Ste. Michelle Indian Wells Columbia Valley Chardonnay 2004. Nice choice. Lovely bottle of wine. But what does the label tell you?

❶ Vintage. The year on the bottle refers to the year the grapes were picked. Can be useful in anticipating freshness, ripeness, etc. but becomes maddening around wine geeks who quote vintages like baseball statistics.

❷ The Varietal. Tells you what grape(s) were used to make the wine. This is mandatory in the U.S. In this case, "Chardonnay" on the label means that at least 75% of the wine's volume is from Chardonnay grapes.

❸ Geographic Origin. This tells you where the grapes were grown to produce the wine. Here the designation is "Columbia Valley," an American Viticultural Area (AVA) from Washington State, meaning that 100% of the grapes came from the Columbia Valley.* By taking note of the geographic origin, you will start to notice the differences in taste from place to place and develop your own preferences for flavor and style of wine. This is the central pleasure of drinking wine.

❹ More Geographic Origin. Names specific vineyards within the AVA. This one names "Indian Wells," so 95% of the grapes must have been grown in this vineyard. Just as the same grape will taste different from state to state and country to country, specific vineyards yield site-specific wines.

❺ The Producer. The naming of names, in this case the estimable Chateau Ste. Michelle. The producer's name is a great harbinger of what is inside. Good producers will produce good wines—even in spotty years.

❻ Alcohol Content. Mandatory on all U.S. wines and a significant clue as to what is inside. Though there is some tolerance allowed in the labeling (plus or minus 1.5%), food-friendly wines tend to range between 12%–15% in alcohol. Lower alcohol levels can indicate some sweetness in the wine, and higher levels can indicate a quick buzz.

The Back Label
❶ The Repeat. Just a quick reminder of what bottle you are holding.

❷ Winemaker's Description. Generally the least helpful part of a label. It can contain further explanations about location and/or technique. Optional by law, required by marketing departments.

❸ More Producer Information. The phrase "Produced and Bottled By" is a legal statement you should take seriously. It means at least 75% of the wine was fermented by the bottler. Taken in conjunction with the other bits of information regarding geographic origins, you can start making some judgments about the wine.

*Laws vary from state to state.

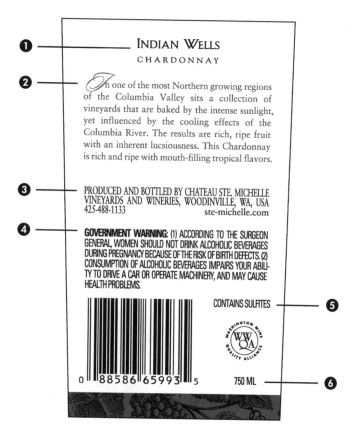

① INDIAN WELLS

CHARDONNAY

② In one of the most Northern growing regions of the Columbia Valley sits a collection of vineyards that are baked by the intense sunlight, yet influenced by the cooling effects of the Columbia River. The results are rich, ripe fruit with an inherent lucsiousness. This Chardonnay is rich and ripe with mouth-filling tropical flavors.

③ PRODUCED AND BOTTLED BY CHATEAU STE. MICHELLE VINEYARDS AND WINERIES, WOODINVILLE, WA, USA
425-488-1133   ste-michelle.com

④ GOVERNMENT WARNING: (1) ACCORDING TO THE SURGEON GENERAL, WOMEN SHOULD NOT DRINK ALCOHOLIC BEVERAGES DURING PREGNANCY BECAUSE OF THE RISK OF BIRTH DEFECTS. (2) CONSUMPTION OF ALCOHOLIC BEVERAGES IMPAIRS YOUR ABILITY TO DRIVE A CAR OR OPERATE MACHINERY, AND MAY CAUSE HEALTH PROBLEMS.

CONTAINS SULFITES **⑤**

0 88586 65993 5

750 ML **⑥**

④ Government Warning. Sadly, there must be a few pregnant women operating heavy equipment who don't know the inherent risks of alcohol consumption. Mandatory on all labels so the government can try to protect people from themselves and subsequent lawsuits.

⑤ Declaration of Sulfites. Sulfites occur naturally during the fermentation process, and most producers dose their wines with sulfites to stabilize them. Some folks are dangerously allergic to sulfites, hence the warning.

⑥ Net Contents. The fluid volume given in metric measurements: 750 ml for a standard bottle, 375 ml for a half bottle, 1.5l for a magnum (double bottle).

French Labels

Much of the information on a bottle of French wine is the same as a domestic one, but there are a few French twists.

Let's take a look at Mssr. Delorme's fine, fine Côtes-du-Rhône from 2004.

❶ Vintage. This is the year the grapes were harvested.

❷ Producer, Part 1: This also can be defined as the name of the wine. However, it is easier to think of it as the producer because, as you will see in just a minute, there are proprietary names that can be associated with a given bottle. Again, this is often the most important clue you'll get about the relative quality of the wine, based on the producer's reputation.

❸ Name of the Wine. Can be fascinating when a winemaker anthropomorphizes a wine but isn't of much use unless the name of the wine has become a brand of its own.

❹ Appellation, Otherwise Known as Geographic Origin.
Here's the biggest difference between domestic and
most European wine labels. While domestic wines are
named by varietal, most European wines are labeled by
the region or vineyard where the grapes come from. The
French Appellation d'Origine Contrôlée certification
system regulates what grapes can be used in what per-
centages in order for a wine to be labeled with a specific
place name or region. However, the more specific the
place name, the more you can determine about any
given bottle. Here, it is the Côtes-du-Rhône. The grapes
could have come from anywhere in the Rhone Valley
in the southeast of France. Knowing this, the next step
is to determine which grapes were used to make the
wine. There are scores of different grapes planted in the
Rhone, but the two dominant red varieties are Grenache
and Syrah. A bit more work? Yes, but after a few times
you'll start to get the hang of it.

❺ Type of Wine. The most basic description of the wine.
Not an indicator of quality. Some of the world's most
interesting wines are simply labeled "Red Table Wine."

❻ Descriptive Information. News for the savvy consumer.
Some information is useful. On this one, "Mis en
Bouteille au Domaine" tells you the wine was bottled
where it was produced—a basic marker of potential
quality. Most is simply marketing jargon.

❼ The Producer, Part 2. Exact information on who made the
wine and where, along with the appellation information
above. Delorme is located in the town of Tavel, and a quick
glance at a map tells you Tavel is in the southern Rhone.
You can then extrapolate that there is a good chance most
of this wine is going to be Grenache, because Grenache
dominates the South, while Syrah rules the North.

❽ Country of Origin. If you are still enjoying "freedom
fries" you might want to look at this information closely.

❾ Alcohol Content. Remember, 12%–15% is food friendly.
Lower alcohol levels imply sweetness, and higher levels
imply a potential hangover.

❿ Net Contents. This is the fluid volume given in metric
measurements: 750 ml for a standard bottle, 375 ml for
a half bottle, 1.5l for a magnum (double bottle).

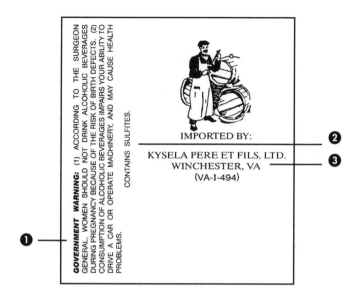

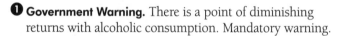

The Back Label

This looks pretty sparse, but there is still something to be gleaned here.

❶ Government Warning. There is a point of diminishing returns with alcoholic consumption. Mandatory warning.

❷ Declaration of Sulfites. Sulfites are naturally occurring in wine. The label must let you know when there is more than 10 parts per million in the bottle.

❸ Name of Importer. Another strong clue as to the relative quality of the bottle in front of you. Some importers do a better job in one region of the world than another, some are known for their quality/value quotient, others are known for managing high-end, difficult-to-find (and afford) bottles. Check the back label each time. See if wines you enjoy come from the same one or two importers. It is just another way to identify which wines you may want to take home and which ones you'll leave on the shelf.

Conclusion

This is just a start. For every rule there is an exception, and each country has different rules and exceptions. Wine can provide for as much further inquiry as you care to take on. So, sample a few bottles, remember what you can, sample a few more, and soon you won't bother drawing straws. You'll already be on the way to the store.

Mark Child is manager at Wine Discount Center in Buffalo Grove

Pairing Wine with Food

by Joe Kafka

Pairing wine with food is not hard; it's just about finding the right combinations.

However, there are a few basic rules to remember. When it comes to flavors, you can either mirror or contrast. For example, match big wines with big foods (like a T-bone steak with Cabernet) and delicate wines with delicate foods (Sauvignon Blanc and green salad comes to mind). On the contrary, pairing an Indian curry dish with a fruity, sweet Riesling provides wonderful balance. And always consider the sauce, not just the meat, when considering the wine.

On the next two pages you'll find a chart illustrating different types of cuisine and wines with which they're well suited. Start with your favorite type of wine, or start with your favorite type of food…either way, you will wind up with complementary flavor profiles to enhance your BYOB dining experience. And remember: think of these as guidelines, not rules, and besides, rules were meant to be broken!

Joe Kafka is the proprietor of KAFKA wine co.

	Asian	BBQ	Chicken	Lamb	Mexican
Albariño					
Barbera					
Barolo				•	
Beaujolais	•				
Cabernet					
Carmenère					
Champagne	•				
Chardonnay			•		
Chianti					
Dessert wines					
Gewürztraminer	•				
Grenache			•		
Malbec					
Merlot					
Muscat					
Pinot Blanc					
Pinot Grigio/Gris			•		•
Pinot Noir			•		
Red Bordeaux					
Riesling	•				•
Rosé					
Sake					
Sauvignon Blanc					
Shiraz/Syrah		•	•		
Tempranillo				•	•
Viognier			•		
White Bordeaux					
Zinfandel		•			

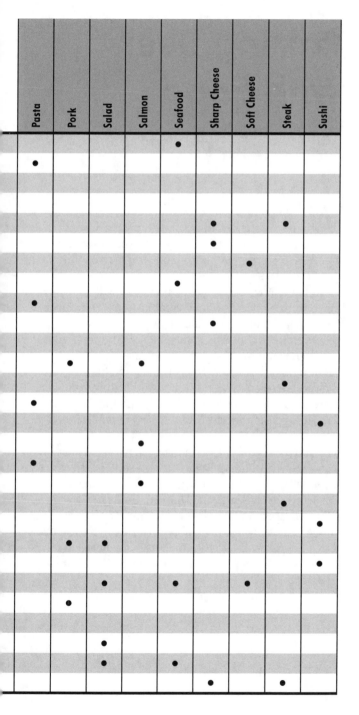

Pairing Beer with Food

by Ray Daniels

Whether you're an expert on microbrews or just enjoy a beer occasionally, you probably know that there are many new beer styles on the market. But when it comes to pairing beer with food, you may be traversing murkier waters.

On the following pages, a pairing chart will help you make winning beer and food combinations. Remember, these are guidelines, not rules. However, pairing the right beer with the right food can heighten your dining experience like you never imagined.

For more information on beer styles and brewing, see the Brewers Association Web site at www.beertown.org. For more information on beer and food events in Chicago, see the Chicago Beer Society Web site at www.chibeer.org.

Ray Daniels is a trained brewmaster, veteran beer writer, and long-time board member of Chicago Beer Society, a beer appreciation group founded in 1977. He is the author of Designing Great Beers: The Ultimate Guide to Brewing Classic Beer Styles *and editor of* The Brewers Association's Guide to Starting Your Own Brewery. *He currently works as director of publications for the Brewers Association and serves on the faculty of the Siebel Institute, Chicago's 130-year-old school of brewing.*

	BBQ: Carolina	BBQ: Kansas City	Cheese: blue veined	Cheese: sharp	Cheese: soft or mild	Cheese: washed rind	Chinese
Alt		●					●
Amber Ale	●						
Amber Lager	●						
American Wheat					●		
Bitter		●				●	
Black Lager/Schwarzbier				●			
Blonde Ale					●		
Bock							
Brown Ale							
Doppelbock	●						
Dubbel						●	
Dunkel						●	
ESB							
Fruit beer					●		
Helles/Dortmunder	●						
Imperial IPA/Barley Wine			●				
IPA				●			●
Kolsch					●		
Lambic						●	
Maibock							
Oktoberfest							
Old Ale				●			
Pale Ale							
Pilsner (all malt)		●					
Porter							
Smoked beer							
Sour Red/Flanders Brown						●	
Spice beer/Holiday beer							
Steam							
Stout, Dry							●
Stout, Foreign or Oatmeal			●				
Stout, Imperial							
Trippel			●				
Vienna					●		
Weizen						●	
Weizenbock							
Wit							

(continued on next page)

	Dessert: cheesecake	Dessert: chocolate	Dessert: custard, flan	Dessert: pumpkin pie	Ethiopian	Ham	Indian	
Alt								
Amber Ale								
Amber Lager								
American Wheat								
Bitter							•	
Black Lager/Schwarzbier			•					
Blonde Ale								
Bock			•			•		
Brown Ale					•			
Doppelbock								
Dubbel								
Dunkel								
ESB							•	
Fruit beer	•							
Helles/Dortmunder								
Imperial IPA/Barley Wine					•			
IPA							•	
Kolsch								
Lambic								
Maibock								
Oktoberfest						•		
Old Ale								
Pale Ale								
Pilsner (all malt)								
Porter					•			
Smoked beer								
Sour Red/Flanders Brown	•							
Spice beer/Holiday beer				•		•		
Steam								
Stout, Dry								
Stout, Foreign or Oatmeal								
Stout, Imperial	•	•						
Trippel								
Vienna								
Weizen								
Weizenbock						•		
Wit								

Mexican	Pasta: cream	Pasta: tomato	Salad: cream dressing	Salad: vinaigrette dressing	Seafood: oysters, shellfish	Seafood: salmon, meaty fish	Seafood: smoked	Seafood: white fish	Steak	Sushi	Thai	Turkey
	•											
				•		•		•				
•										•		
				•							•	
•			•									
										•		
						•						
							•					•
							•					
									•			
				•								
								•				
			•									
	•								•			
				•					•			
			•					•				
	•											
					•				•			
							•					•
		•				•			•			
		•			•							
							•					
			•									•
•		•								•		
											•	
							•					
	•	•	•								•	

Indexes

CHICAGO

BYOB Restaurants by Cuisine

AFGHAN
Afghan Restaurant / *West Rogers Park*
Kabul House / *Evanston*

AFRICAN
BQ Afro Root Cuisine / *Uptown*

AMERICAN
Ann Sather / *Lakeview (3 locations)*
The Bagel / *Lakeview*
Buzz Café / *Oak Park*
Caffe Florian / *Hyde Park*
C'est Si Bon / *Hyde Park*
Cold Comfort Café / *Wicker Park*
5 Loaves Eatery / *South Shore*
Feed / *Humboldt Park*
Healthy Food Lithuanian Restaurant / *Bridgeport*
Medici on 57th / *Hyde Park*
Nookies Tree / *Lakeview*
Nookies / *Old Town*
Nookies Too / *Lincoln Park*
North Coast Café / *Lakeview*
Over Easy Café / *Ravenswood*
Robinson's No. 1 Ribs Lincoln Park / *Lincoln Park*

ARGENTINIAN
Buenos Aires Forever / *Noble Square*
Fierros / *Lakeview*
Tango Sur / *Lakeview*

BBQ
Calvin's BBQ / *Logan Square*
Robinson's No. 1 Ribs Lincoln Park / *Lincoln Park*
Tripi's Joint / *Lakeview*

BRUNCH
Adesso / *Lakeview*
Ann Sather / *Lakeview* (3 *locations*)
Bite Café / *Ukrainian Village*
Bon Soiree / *Logan Square*
Buzz Café / *Oak Park*
Café Too / *Uptown*
Caffe Florian / *Hyde Park*
C'est Si Bon / *Hyde Park*
Cold Comfort Café / *Wicker Park*
Crepes on Broadway / *Lakeview*
Flying Saucer / *Humboldt Park*
HB / *Lakeview*
Karyn's / *Lincoln Park*
Los Nopales / *Lincoln Square*
M. Henry / *Edgewater*
Mamacita's / *Lincoln Park*
Medici on 57th / *Hyde Park*
Nookies Tree / *Lakeview*
Nookies / *Old Town*
Nookies Too / *Lincoln Park*
North Coast Café / *Lakeview*
Orange / *Lakeview*
Orange / *South Loop*
Over Easy Café / *Ravenswood*
Papacito's Mexican Grille / *Lakeview*
Rique's Regional Mexican Food / *Uptown*
Taboun Grill / *West Rogers Park*
Tre Kronor / *Albany Park*
Treat / *Humboldt Park*
Wrightwood Skewers & Café / *Logan Square*

CAFÉ
Atlas Café / *Logan Square*
Buzz Café / *Oak Park*

CARIBBEAN
Cafe Central / *West Town*
Café Trinidad / *Chatham*
Rhythm and Spice / *South Shore*
Rudy's Taste / *East Ukrainian Village*

CHINESE

Ba Mien Viet Food Court / *Uptown*
Bamboo Garden / *Lakeview*
China Café Seafood Restaurant / *Chinatown*
Chinoiserie / *Wilmette*
Dragon King / *Chinatown*
Friendship Restaurant / *Logan Square*
Golden Bull / *Chinatown*
Luc Thang / *Wicker Park*
Mandarin Kitchen / *Chinatown*
Mark's Chop Suey / *Lakeview*
Mei Shung / *Edgewater*
Nan's Sushi & Chinese / *Lincoln Park*
New Jeanny's Restaurant / *Lakeview*
Phoenix Inn / *Evanston*
Pinto Thai Kitchen / *Evanston*
Shui Wah / *Chinatown*
Spring World / *Chinatown*
Tien Giang / *Uptown*
Vien Dong / *Lakeview*
Yang Restaurant / *South Loop*

CONTEMPORARY AMERICAN

HB / *Lakeview*
M. Henry / *Edgewater*
Orange / *Lakeview*
State Restaurant and Café / *Lincoln Park*
Think / *Bucktown*

COSTA RICAN

Irazu / *Wicker Park*
Palmito's / *Lakeview*

CREPES

Crepes on Broadway / *Lakeview*

CUBAN

Sabor A Cuba / *Lincoln Square*

ECLECTIC
Atlas Café / *Logan Square*
Bite Café / *Ukrainian Village*
Bon Soiree / *Logan Square*
Café Society / *Prairie District*
Café Too / *Uptown*
CHIC Café / *River North*
Flying Saucer / *Humboldt Park*
Hot Doug's / *Irving Park*
May St. Café / *Pilsen*
Orange / *Lakeview*
Orange / *South Loop*
Schwa / *Wicker Park*
Speakeasy Supper Club / *Edgewater*
Treat / *Humboldt Park*
Wrightwood Skewers & Café / *Logan Square*

ECUADORIAN
La Sierra / *Ravenswood*

ETHIOPIAN
Queen of Sheba Café / *Edgewater*

FRENCH
Rick's Café Casablanca / *Lakeview*

FUSION
Think / *Bucktown*

GREEK
Greek Corner / *Ukrainian Village*

GUATEMALAN
Rudy's Taste / *East Ukrainian Village*

INDIAN
Bhabi's Kitchen / *West Rogers Park*
Curry House / *Lincoln Park*
Hema's Kitchen / *West Rogers Park*
Hema's Kitchen II / *Lincoln Park*

Indian Grill / *Lincoln Park*
Mysore Woodlands / *West Rogers Park*
Passage to India / *Lincoln Square*
Sher-A-Punjab / *West Rogers Park*
Standard India / *Lakeview*
Udupi Palace / *West Rogers Park*

ISRAELI
Hashalom / *West Rogers Park*
Taboun Grill / *West Rogers Park*

ITALIAN
Adesso / *Lakeview*
Caffe Florian / *Hyde Park*
Caro Mio Italian Ristorante / *Ravenswood*
Edwardo's / *Hyde Park*
Gino's East / *Lakeview*
Gio's Café and Deli / *Bridgeport*
La Cucina di Donatella / *West Rogers Park*
Lucia Ristorante / *Wicker Park*
Pizza Rustica / *Lakeview*
Ranalli's Up North / *Uptown*
Rick's Café Casablanca / *Lakeview*
Rosati's / *River North*
Terragusto / *Lakeview*
Think / *Bucktown*
Trattoria Caterina / *South Loop*
Villa Rosa Pizza & Pasta / *Edgebrook*
Wise Guys / *Logan Square*

JAMAICAN
Jamaica Gates Restaurant / *Evanston*
Rhythm and Spice / *South Shore*

JAPANESE
Asian Avenue / *Lakeview*
Butterfly Sushi Bar & Thai Cuisine / *River West*
Café Blossom / *Lakeview*
Café Furaibo / *Lakeview*
Café Sushi / *Old Town*
Coast Sushi Bar / *Bucktown*

Hama Matsu / *Andersonville*
Indie Café / *Rogers Park*
Japonica / *University Village/Little Italy*
Katachi / *Lakeview*
Kikuya / *Hyde Park*
Lincoln Park's Noodle House / *Lincoln Park*
Matsu Yama / *Lakeview*
New Tokyo / *Lakeview*
Sunshine Café / *Andersonville*
Sushi 28 Café / *Lakeview*
Sushi II Para / *Lincoln Park*
Thai Oscar / *Lincoln Square*

JEWISH
The Bagel / *Lakeview*
Cold Comfort Café / *Wicker Park*

KOREAN
Café Corea / *Hyde Park*
Hama Matsu / *Andersonville*
Kokeeri Restaurant / *Mayfair*
San Chae Dol Sot Restaurant / *Albany Park*
So Gong Dong Tofu Restaurant / *North Park*

LAOTIAN
Nhu Hoa Café / *Uptown*

LITHUANIAN
Healthy Food Lithuanian Restaurant / *Bridgeport*

MEDITERRANEAN
Cedar's Mediterranean Kitchen / *Hyde Park*
Marrakech Cuisine / *Noble Square*
Olive Mountain / *Evanston*
Sinbad's Fine Mediterranean Grill / *Lincoln Park*
Sultan's Market / *Wicker Park*

MEXICAN

Buena Vista Restaurant / *Lakeview*
Caliente / *Lakeview*
Caliente / *Logan Square*
Dorado / *Ravenswood*
El Presidente / *Lincoln Park*
La Cazuela Mariscos / *Rogers Park*
La Sierra / *Ravenswood*
Los Nopales / *Lincoln Square*
Mamacita's / *Lincoln Park*
Nuevo Léon Restaurant / *Pilsen*
Papacito's Mexican Grille / *Lakeview*
Ranalli's Up North / *Uptown*
Rique's Regional Mexican Food / *Uptown*
Rudy's Taste / *East Ukrainian Village*
Sol de Mexico / *Cragin*
Wholly Frijoles / *Lincolnwood*

MIDDLE EASTERN

Casbah Café / *Lakeview*
Fattoush / *Lincoln Park*
Kan Zaman / *River North*
Nile Restaurant / *Hyde Park*
Old Jerusalem Restaurant / *Old Town*
Semiramis / *Albany Park*
Sultan's Market / *Wicker Park*
Taboun Grill / *West Rogers Park*

MOROCCAN

Andalous Moroccan / *Lakeview*
Hashalom / *West Rogers Park*
Marrakech Cuisine / *Noble Square*
Tagine / *Ravenswood*

NUEVO LATINO

May St. Café / *Pilsen*

PAKISTANI
Bhabi's Kitchen / *West Rogers Park*

PAN-ASIAN
Blue Elephant / *Edgewater*
Cozy Noodles & Rice / *Lakeview*
Cozy Noodles & Rice / *Evanston*
Ecce Café / *Lakeview*
Fan Si Pan / *East Ukrainian Village*
Joy Yee Noodle / *Evanston*
Joy Yee Noodle / *Chinatown*
Joy Yee Noodle / *University Village*
Noodles Etc. / *Hyde Park* (2 locations)
Oodles of Noodles / *Lincoln Park*
Penny's Noodle Shop / *Lakeview*
Pingpong / *Lakeview*
Satay / *Lakeview*
Thai Grill / *Edgewater*
Zen Noodles / *Bucktown*

PERUVIAN
Ay Ay Picante / *Mayfair*
Taste of Peru / *Rogers Park*

PIZZA
Edwardo's / *Hyde Park*
Gino's East / *Lakeview*
Pizza Rustica / *Lakeview*
Ranalli's Up North / *Uptown*
Rosati's / *River North*
Villa Rosa Pizza & Pasta / *Edgebrook*
Wise Guys / *Logan Square*

PUERTO RICAN
Borinquen / *Humboldt Park*
Cafe Central / *West Town*
La Cocina de Galarza Restaurant / *Logan Square*

SCANDINAVIAN
Ann Sather / *Lakeview* (3 locations)
Tre Kronor / *Albany Park*

SOUTH AMERICAN
Caracas Grill / *Rogers Park*
El Llano Restaurant / *Lakeview*
El Llano Restaurant / *Rogers Park*

SUSHI
Asian Avenue / *Lakeview*
Butterfly Sushi Bar & Thai Cuisine / *River West*
Café Blossom / *Lakeview*
Café Furaibo / *Lakeview*
Café Sushi / *Old Town*
Coast Sushi Bar / *Bucktown*
Ecce Café / *Lakeview*
Grande Noodles & Sushi Bar / *Rogers Park*
Hama Matsu / *Andersonville*
Indie Café / *Rogers Park*
Jai-Yen Fusion Restaurant / *Lakeview*
Japonica / *University Village/Little Italy*
J-Thai Sushi Bar and Thai Cuisine / *Lakeview*
Katachi / *Lakeview*
Kikuya / *Hyde Park*
Lincoln Park's Noodle House / *Lincoln Park*
Matsu Yama / *Lakeview*
Nan's Sushi & Chinese / *Lincoln Park*
New Tokyo / *Lakeview*
Noodle Zone / *Andersonville*
Satay / *Lakeview*
Sushi 28 Café / *Lakeview*
Sushi II Para / *Lincoln Park*
Sushi X / *River West*
Tanoshii / *Edgewater*
Thai Lagoon / *Bucktown*
Thai Oscar / *Lincoln Square*
Thai Spice / *Rogers Park*
Tom Yum Thai Cuisine / *Albany Park*
Toro Sushi / *Lincoln Park*
T-Spot Sushi and Tea Bar / *North Center*
Wakamono / *Lakeview*
Zen Noodles / *Bucktown*

TAIWANESE
Mei Shung / *Edgewater*

THAI

Always Thai / *North Center*
Aroy Thai / *Ravenswood*
Asian Avenue / *Lakeview*
At Café / *West Rogers Park*
Azha / *Lakeview*
Barberry Pan Asian Kitchen / *Lakeview*
Butterfly Sushi Bar & Thai Cuisine / *River West*
Café Hoang / *Uptown*
Charley Thai Place / *Logan Square*
Duck Walk / *Lakeview*
The Elephant / *Edgebrook*
EN•THAI•CE / *Edgewater*
Garlic & Chili / *Old Town*
Grande Noodles & Sushi Bar / *Rogers Park*
Indie Café / *Rogers Park*
Jai-Yen Fusion Restaurant / *Lakeview*
Jasmine Rice / *Belmont Central*
Jim Noodle & Rice / *Lakeview*
Jitlada Thai House / *Lakeview*
Joy's Noodles & Rice / *Lakeview*
J-Thai Sushi Bar and Thai Cuisine / *Lakeview*
Lincoln Park's Noodle House / *Lincoln Park*
Luc Thang / *Wicker Park*
Mr. Thai / *Lakeview*
Noodle Zone / *Andersonville*
Noodles in the Pot / *Lincoln Park*
Opart Thai House / *Lincoln Square*
P.S. Bangkok 2 / *Lincoln Park*
Panang / *Near North*
Pinto Thai Kitchen / *Evanston*
Pot Pan / *Bucktown*
Preaw Whan / *Uptown*
Roong Petch / *Lincoln Square*
Rosded / *Lincoln Square*
Royal Thai / *Lincoln Square*
Ruby of Siam / *Skokie*
Sai Mai Thai Restaurant / *Logan Square*
Siam Country / *Lincoln Square*
Siam Noodle & Rice / *Uptown*
Siam Rice Thai Cuisine / *Loop*
Siam Taste Noodle / *Old Irving Park*
Snail Thai Cuisine / *Hyde Park*

The Spice Thai Cuisine / *Logan Square*
Spoon Thai / *Lincoln Square*
Sticky Rice / *North Center*
Sweet Tamarind / *Lakeview*
Thai 55 / *Hyde Park*
Thai Aree / *Old Irving Park*
Thai Aroma / *Uptown*
Thai Aroma / *Old Town*
Thai Avenue / *Uptown*
Thai Classic / *Lakeview*
Thai Eatery / *Logan Square*
Thai Grill / *Edgewater*
Thai Kitchen / *Lakeview*
Thai Lagoon / *Bucktown*
Thai Linda Café / *Roscoe Village*
Thai Me Up / *Lakeview*
Thai on Clark / *Ravenswood*
Thai Oscar / *Lincoln Square*
Thai Pastry / *Uptown*
Thai Spice / *Rogers Park*
Thai Valley / *Albany Park*
Thai Village / *Wicker Park*
Tom Yum Thai Cuisine / *Albany Park*
Tub Tim Thai / *Skokie*
Yes Thai / *Lincoln Square*

TURKISH
Turkish Cuisine & Bakery / *Edgewater*

VEGETARIAN-FRIENDLY
Afghan Restaurant / *West Rogers Park*
Andalous Moroccan / *Lakeview*
Atlas Café / *Logan Square*
Ba Mien Viet Food Court / *Uptown*
Bamboo Garden / *Lakeview*
Bite Café / *Ukrainian Village*
Caro Mio Italian Ristorante / *Ravenswood*
Cedar's Mediterranean Kitchen / *Hyde Park*
EN•THAI•CE / *Edgewater*
Fattoush / *Lincoln Park*
Flying Saucer / *Humboldt Park*
Hema's Kitchen / *West Rogers Park*

Hema's Kitchen II / *Lincoln Park*
Jim Noodle & Rice / *Lakeview*
Karyn's / *Lincoln Park*
Mamacita's / *Lincoln Park*
Mysore Woodlands / *West Rogers Park*
Old Jerusalem Restaurant / *Old Town*
Passage to India / *Lincoln Square*
Phoenix Inn / *Evanston*
Pot Pan / *Bucktown*
Queen of Sheba Café / *Edgewater*
Royal Thai / *Lincoln Square*
Siam Taste Noodle / *Old Irving Park*
The Spice Thai Cuisine / *Logan Square*
Standard India / *Lakeview*
Sultan's Market / *Wicker Park*
Thai Grill / *Edgewater*
Udupi Palace / *West Rogers Park*

VIETNAMESE

Ba Mien Viet Food Court / *Uptown*
Ben Tre Café & Restaurant / *West Rogers Park*
Café Hoang / *Uptown*
Café Lao / *Uptown*
Fan Si Pan / *East Ukrainian Village*
Hoang Thanh / *Uptown*
Luc Thang / *Wicker Park*
Nhu Hoa Café / *Uptown*
The Noodle / *Chinatown*
Pho 888 / *Uptown*
Tank Restaurant / *Uptown*
Thai Binh / *Uptown*
Tien Giang / *Uptown*
Vien Dong / *Lakeview*

BYOB Restaurants by Location

ALBANY PARK
San Chae Dol Sot Restaurant / *Korean*
Semiramis / *Middle Eastern*
Thai Valley / *Thai*
Tom Yum Thai Cuisine / *Thai, Sushi*
Tre Kronor / *Scandinavian, Brunch*

ANDERSONVILLE
Hama Matsu / *Sushi, Japanese, Korean*
Noodle Zone / *Thai, Sushi*
Sunshine Café / *Japanese*

BELMONT CENTRAL
Jasmine Rice / *Thai*

BRIDGEPORT
Gio's Café and Deli / *Italian*
Healthy Food Lithuanian Restaurant / *Lithuanian, American*

BUCKTOWN
Coast Sushi Bar / *Sushi, Japanese*
Pot Pan / *Thai, Vegetarian-Friendly*
Thai Lagoon / *Thai, Sushi*
Think / *Contemporary American, Fusion, Italian*
Zen Noodles / *Pan-Asian, Sushi*

CHATHAM
Café Trinidad / *Caribbean*

CHINATOWN
China Café Seafood Restaurant / *Chinese*
Dragon King / *Chinese*
Golden Bull / *Chinese*

Joy Yee Noodle / *Pan-Asian*
Mandarin Kitchen / *Chinese*
The Noodle / *Vietnamese*
Shui Wah / *Chinese*
Spring World / *Chinese*

CRAGIN
Sol de Mexico / *Mexican*

EAST UKRAINIAN VILLAGE
Fan Si Pan / *Pan-Asian, Vietnamese*
Rudy's Taste / *Caribbean, Guatemalan, Mexican*

EDGEBROOK
The Elephant / *Thai*
Villa Rosa Pizza & Pasta / *Italian, Pizza*

EDGEWATER
Blue Elephant / *Pan-Asian*
EN•THAI•CE / *Thai, Vegetarian-Friendly*
M. Henry / *Contemporary American, Brunch*
Mei Shung / *Taiwanese, Chinese*
Queen of Sheba Café / *Ethiopian, Vegetarian-Friendly*
Speakeasy Supper Club / *Eclectic*
Tanoshii / *Sushi*
Thai Grill / *Thai, Pan-Asian, Vegetarian-Friendly*
Turkish Cuisine & Bakery / *Turkish*

EVANSTON
Cozy Noodles & Rice / *Pan-Asian*
Jamaica Gates Restaurant / *Jamaican*
Joy Yee Noodle / *Pan-Asian*
Kabul House / *Afghan*
Olive Mountain / *Mediterranean*
Phoenix Inn / *Chinese, Vegetarian-Friendly*
Pinto Thai Kitchen / *Thai, Chinese*

HUMBOLDT PARK
Borinquen / *Puerto Rican*
Feed / *American*

Flying Saucer / *Eclectic, Vegetarian-Friendly, Brunch*
Treat / *Eclectic, Brunch*

HYDE PARK
Café Corea / *Korean*
Caffe Florian / *Italian, American, Brunch*
Cedar's Mediterranean Kitchen / *Mediterranean, Vegetarian-Friendly*
C'est Si Bon / *American, Brunch*
Edwardo's / *Italian, Pizza*
Kikuya / *Japanese, Sushi*
Medici on 57th / *American, Brunch*
Nile Restaurant / *Middle Eastern*
Noodles Etc. (2 locations) / *Pan-Asian*
Snail Thai Cuisine / *Thai*
Thai 55 / *Thai*

IRVING PARK
Hot Doug's / *Eclectic*

LAKEVIEW
Adesso / *Brunch, Italian*
Andalous Moroccan / *Moroccan, Vegetarian-Friendly*
Ann Sather (3 locations) / *Scandinavian, American, Brunch*
Asian Avenue / *Sushi, Japanese, Thai*
Azha / *Thai*
The Bagel / *Jewish, American*
Bamboo Garden / *Chinese, Vegetarian-Friendly*
Barberry Pan Asian Kitchen / *Thai*
Buena Vista Restaurant / *Mexican*
Café Blossom / *Sushi, Japanese*
Café Furaibo / *Sushi, Japanese*
Caliente / *Mexican*
Casbah Café / *Middle Eastern*
Cozy Noodles & Rice / *Pan-Asian*
Crepes on Broadway / *Crepes, Brunch*
Duck Walk / *Thai*
Ecce Café / *Pan-Asian, Sushi*
El Llano Restaurant / *South American*
Fierros / *Argentinian*
Gino's East / *Italian, Pizza*
HB / *Contemporary American, Brunch*
Jai-Yen Fusion Restaurant / *Sushi, Thai*

Jim Noodle & Rice / *Thai, Vegetarian-Friendly*
Jitlada Thai House / *Thai*
Joy's Noodles & Rice / *Thai*
J-Thai Sushi Bar and Thai Cuisine / *Sushi, Thai*
Katachi / *Sushi, Japanese*
Mr. Thai / *Thai*
Mark's Chop Suey / *Chinese*
Matsu Yama / *Japanese, Sushi*
New Jeanny's Restaurant / *Chinese*
New Tokyo / *Sushi, Japanese*
Nookies Tree / *American, Brunch*
North Coast Café / *American, Brunch*
Orange / *Brunch, Contemporary American, Eclectic*
Palmito's / *Costa Rican*
Papacito's Mexican Grille / *Mexican, Brunch*
Penny's Noodle Shop / *Pan-Asian*
Pingpong / *Pan-Asian*
Pizza Rustica / *Italian, Pizza*
Rick's Café Casablanca / *French, Italian*
Satay / *Pan-Asian, Sushi*
Standard India / *Indian, Vegetarian-Friendly*
Sushi 28 Café / *Sushi, Japanese*
Sweet Tamarind / *Thai*
Tango Sur / *Argentinian*
Terragusto / *Italian*
Thai Classic / *Thai*
Thai Kitchen / *Thai*
Thai Me Up / *Thai*
Tripi's Joint / *BBQ*
Vien Dong / *Vietnamese, Chinese*
Wakamono / *Sushi*

LINCOLN PARK
Curry House / *Indian*
El Presidente / *Mexican*
Fattoush / *Middle Eastern, Vegetarian-Friendly*
Hema's Kitchen II / *Indian, Vegetarian-Friendly*
Indian Grill / *Indian*
Karyn's / *Vegetarian-Friendly, Brunch*
Lincoln Park's Noodle House / *Thai, Japanese, Sushi*
Mamacita's / *Mexican, Vegetarian-Friendly, Brunch*
Nan's Sushi & Chinese / *Chinese, Sushi*
Noodles in the Pot / *Thai*

Nookies Too / *American, Brunch*
Oodles of Noodles / *Pan-Asian*
P.S. Bangkok 2 / *Thai*
Robinson's No. 1 Ribs Lincoln Park / *BBQ, American*
Sinbad's Fine Mediterranean Grill / *Mediterranean*
State Restaurant & Café / *Contemporary American*
Sushi II Para / *Japanese, Sushi*
Toro Sushi / *Sushi*

LINCOLN SQUARE

Los Nopales / *Mexican, Brunch*
Opart Thai House / *Thai*
Passage to India / *Indian, Vegetarian-Friendly*
Roong Petch / *Thai*
Rosded / *Thai*
Royal Thai / *Thai, Vegetarian-Friendly*
Sabor A Cuba / *Cuban*
Siam Country / *Thai*
Spoon Thai / *Thai*
Thai Oscar / *Japanese, Sushi, Thai*
Yes Thai / *Thai*

LINCOLNWOOD

Wholly Frijoles / *Mexican*

LOGAN SQUARE

Atlas Café / *Café, Eclectic, Vegetarian-Friendly*
Bon Soiree / *Eclectic, Brunch*
Caliente / *Mexican*
Calvin's BBQ / *BBQ*
Charley Thai Place / *Thai*
Friendship Restaurant / *Chinese*
La Cocina de Galarza Restaurant / *Puerto Rican*
Sai Mai Thai Restaurant / *Thai*
The Spice Thai Cuisine / *Thai, Vegetarian-Friendly*
Thai Eatery / *Thai*
Wise Guys / *Italian, Pizza*
Wrightwood Skewers & Café / *Eclectic, Brunch*

LOOP

Siam Rice Thai Cuisine / *Thai*

MAYFAIR
Ay Ay Picante / *Peruvian*
Kokeeri Restaurant / *Korean*

NEAR NORTH
Panang / *Thai*

NOBLE SQUARE
Buenos Aires Forever / *Argentinian*
Marrakech Cuisine / *Moroccan, Mediterranean*

NORTH CENTER
Always Thai / *Thai*
Sticky Rice / *Thai*
T-Spot Sushi and Tea Bar / *Sushi*

NORTH PARK
So Gong Dong Tofu Restaurant / *Korean*

OAK PARK
Buzz Café / *American, Café, Brunch*

OLD IRVING PARK
Siam Taste Noodle / *Thai, Vegetarian-Friendly*
Thai Aree / *Thai*

OLD TOWN
Café Sushi / *Sushi, Japanese*
Garlic & Chili / *Thai*
Nookies / *American, Brunch*
Old Jerusalem Restaurant / *Middle Eastern, Vegetarian-Friendly*
Thai Aroma / *Thai*

PILSEN
May St. Café / *Nuevo Latino, Eclectic*
Nuevo Léon Restaurant / *Mexican*

PRAIRIE DISTRICT
Café Society / *Eclectic*

RAVENSWOOD

Aroy Thai / *Thai*
Caro Mio Italian Ristorante / *Italian, Vegetarian-Friendly*
Dorado / *Mexican*
La Sierra / *Mexican, Ecuadorian*
Over Easy Café / *American, Brunch*
Tagine / *Moroccan*
Thai on Clark / *Thai*

RIVER NORTH

CHIC Café / *Eclectic*
Kan Zaman / *Middle Eastern*
Rosati's / *Pizza, Italian*

RIVER WEST

Butterfly Sushi Bar & Thai Cuisine / *Sushi, Thai, Japanese*
Sushi X / *Sushi*

ROGERS PARK

Caracas Grill / *South American*
El Llano Restaurant / *South American*
Grande Noodles & Sushi Bar / *Sushi, Thai*
Indie Café / *Sushi, Japanese, Thai*
La Cazuela Mariscos / *Mexican*
Taste of Peru / *Peruvian*
Thai Spice / *Thai, Sushi*

ROSCOE VILLAGE

Thai Linda Café / *Thai*

SKOKIE

Ruby of Siam / *Thai*
Tub Tim Thai / *Thai*

SOUTH LOOP

Orange / *Brunch, Eclectic*
Trattoria Caterina / *Italian*
Yang Restaurant / *Chinese*

SOUTH SHORE
5 Loaves Eatery / *American*
Rhythm and Spice / *Jamaican, Caribbean*

UKRAINIAN VILLAGE
Bite Café / *Eclectic, Vegetarian-Friendly, Brunch*
Greek Corner / *Greek*

UNIVERSITY VILLAGE/LITTLE ITALY
Japonica / *Sushi, Japanese*
Joy Yee Noodle / *Pan-Asian*

UPTOWN
BQ Afro Root Cuisine / *African*
Ba Mien Viet Food Court / *Vietnamese, Chinese, Vegetarian-Friendly*
Café Hoang / *Vietnamese, Thai*
Café Lao / *Vietnamese*
Café Too / *Eclectic, Brunch*
Hoang Thanh / *Vietnamese*
Nhu Hoa Café / *Vietnamese, Laotian*
Pho 888 / *Vietnamese*
Preaw Whan / *Thai*
Ranalli's Up North / *Italian, Pizza, Mexican*
Rique's Regional Mexican Food / *Mexican, Brunch*
Siam Noodle & Rice / *Thai*
Tank Restaurant / *Vietnamese*
Thai Aroma / *Thai*
Thai Avenue / *Thai*
Thai Binh / *Vietnamese*
Thai Pastry / *Thai*
Tien Giang / *Vietnamese, Chinese*

WEST ROGERS PARK
Afghan Restaurant / *Afghan, Vegetarian-Friendly*
At Café / *Thai*
Ben Tre Café & Restaurant / *Vietnamese*
Bhabi's Kitchen / *Indian, Pakistani*
Hashalom Restaurant / *Israeli, Moroccan*
Hema's Kitchen / *Indian, Vegetarian-Friendly*
La Cucina di Donatella / *Italian*
Mysore Woodlands / *Indian, Vegetarian-Friendly*

Sher-A-Punjab / *Indian*
Taboun Grill / *Middle Eastern, Israeli, Brunch*
Udupi Palace / *Indian, Vegetarian-Friendly*

WEST TOWN
Cafe Central / *Puerto Rican, Caribbean*

WICKER PARK
Cold Comfort Café / *American, Jewish, Brunch*
Irazu / *Costa Rican*
Luc Thang / *Thai, Chinese, Vietnamese*
Lucia Ristorante / *Italian*
Schwa / *Eclectic*
Sultan's Market / *Middle Eastern, Mediterranean, Vegetarian-Friendly*
Thai Village / *Thai*

WILMETTE
Chinoiserie / *Chinese*

BYOB Restaurants by Feature

OUTDOOR SEATING
Andalous Moroccan (*Lakeview, Moroccan/Vegetarian-Friendly*)
Ann Sather (*Lakeview/Southport, Scandinavian/American/Brunch*)
Blue Elephant (*Edgewater, Pan-Asian*)
Butterfly Sushi Bar & Thai Cuisine (*River West, Sushi/Thai/Japanese*)
Buzz Café (*Oak Park, American/Café/Brunch*)
Café Blossom (*Lakeview, Sushi/Japanese*)
Café Sushi (*Old Town, Sushi/Japanese*)
Café Too (*Uptown, Eclectic/Brunch*)
Caliente (*Lakeview, Mexican*)
Calvin's BBQ (*Logan Square, BBQ*)
Caro Mio Italian Ristorante (*Ravenswood, Italian/Vegetarian-
    Friendly*

Chinoiserie (*Wilmette, Chinese*)
Cold Comfort Café (*Wicker Park, American/Jewish/Brunch*)
Cozy Noodles & Rice (*Lakeview, Pan-Asian*)
Ecce Café (*Lakeview, Pan-Asian/Sushi*)
El Presidente (*Lincoln Park, Mexican*)
EN•THAI•CE (*Edgewater, Thai/Vegetarian-Friendly*)
5 Loaves Eatery (*South Shore, American*)
Feed (*Humboldt Park, American*)
Gino's East (*Lakeview, Italian/Pizza*)
Greek Corner (*Ukrainian Village, Greek*)
Irazu (*Wicker Park, Costa Rican*)
Jim Noodle & Rice (*Lakeview, Thai/Vegetarian-Friendly*)
Jitlada Thai House (*Lakeview, Thai*)
Joy's Noodles & Rice (*Lakeview, Thai*)
Joy Yee Noodle (*Evanston, Pan-Asian*)
J-Thai Sushi Bar and Thai Cuisine (*Lakeview, Sushi/Thai*)
Kan Zaman (*River North, Middle Eastern*)
Karyn's (*Lincoln Park, Vegetarian-Friendly/Brunch*)
Katachi (*Lakeview, Sushi/Japanese*)
La Cazuela Mariscos (*Rogers Park, Mexican*)
La Cocina de Galarza Restaurant (*Logan Square, Puerto Rican*)
La Cucina di Donatella (*West Rogers Park, Italian*)
Lucia Ristorante (*Wicker Park, Italian*)
M. Henry (*Edgewater, Contemporary American/Brunch*)
Medici on 57th (*Hyde Park, American/Brunch*)
New Tokyo (*Lakeview, Sushi/Japanese*)
Noodles in the Pot (*Lincoln Park, Thai*)
Nookies Tree (*Lakeview, American/Brunch*)
Nookies (*Old Town, American/Brunch*)
North Coast Café (*Lakeview, American/Brunch*)
Old Jerusalem Restaurant (*Old Town, Middle Eastern/Vegetarian-Friendly*)
Orange (*Lakeview, Brunch/Contemporary American/Eclectic*)
Panang (*Near North, Thai*)
Penny's Noodle Shop (*Lakeview, Pan-Asian*)
Pingpong (*Lakeview, Pan-Asian*)
Pizza Rustica (*Lakeview, Italian/Pizza*)
Ranalli's Up North (*Uptown, Italian/Pizza/Mexican*)
Rick's Café Casablanca (*Lakeview, French/Italian*)
Robinson's No. 1 Ribs Lincoln Park (*Lincoln Park, BBQ/American*)
Rosati's (*River North, Pizza/Italian*)
Sabor A Cuba (*Lincoln Square, Cuban*)
Siam Country (*Lincoln Square, Thai*)

Sinbad's Fine Mediterranean Grill (*Lincoln Park, Mediterranean*)
Sultan's Market (*Wicker Park, Middle Eastern/Mediterranean/ Vegetarian-Friendly*)
Sweet Tamarind (*Lakeview, Thai*)
Tagine (*Ravenswood, Moroccan*)
Tango Sur (*Lakeview, Argentinian*)
Terragusto (*Lakeview, Italian*)
Thai Linda Café (*Roscoe Village, Thai*)
Thai Pastry (*Uptown, Thai*)
Thai Village (*Wicker Park, Thai*)
Think (*Bucktown, Contemporary American/Fusion/Italian*)
Trattoria Caterina (*South Loop, Italian*)
Tre Kronor (*Albany Park, Scandinavian/Brunch*)
Wakamono (*Lakeview, Sushi*)
Wrightwood Skewers & Cafe (*Logan Square, Eclectic/Brunch*)
Yes Thai (*Lincoln Square, Thai*)

LIVE ENTERTAINMENT

Always Thai (*North Center, Thai*)
Atlas Café (*Logan Square, Café/Eclectic/Vegetarian-Friendly*)
Ba Mien Viet Food Court (*Uptown, Vietnamese/Chinese/Vegetarian-Friendly*)
5 Loaves Eatery (*South Shore, American*)
Kan Zaman (*River North, Middle Eastern*)
Marrakech Cuisine (*Noble Square, Moroccan/Mediterranean*)
Speakeasy Supper Club (*Edgewater, Eclectic*)
Taste of Peru (*Rogers Park, Peruvian*)
Turkish Cuisine & Bakery (*Edgewater, Turkish*)
Wrightwood Skewers & Café (*Logan Square, Eclectic/Brunch*)

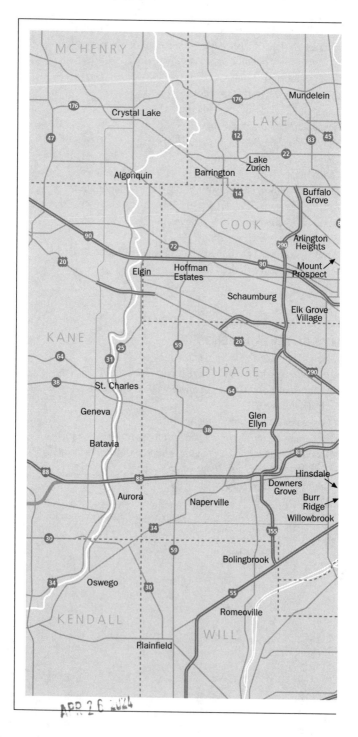

Chicago Neighborhoods

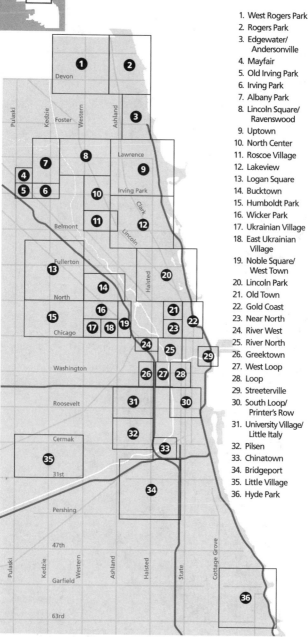

1. West Rogers Park
2. Rogers Park
3. Edgewater/ Andersonville
4. Mayfair
5. Old Irving Park
6. Irving Park
7. Albany Park
8. Lincoln Square/ Ravenswood
9. Uptown
10. North Center
11. Roscoe Village
12. Lakeview
13. Logan Square
14. Bucktown
15. Humboldt Park
16. Wicker Park
17. Ukrainian Village
18. East Ukrainian Village
19. Noble Square/ West Town
20. Lincoln Park
21. Old Town
22. Gold Coast
23. Near North
24. River West
25. River North
26. Greektown
27. West Loop
28. Loop
29. Streeterville
30. South Loop/ Printer's Row
31. University Village/ Little Italy
32. Pilsen
33. Chinatown
34. Bridgeport
35. Little Village
36. Hyde Park